ENCYCLOPEDIA

Porcelain Enamel Advertising

with Price Guide

Revised and Expanded 2nd Edition

Michael Bruner

4880 Lower Valley Road, Atglen, PA 19310 USA

DEDICATION

To my father ERWIN J. BRUNER (1903–1992)

SPECIAL THANKS AND ACKNOWLEDGMENTS

As with any worthwhile endeavor, certain key people have made a lot of difference in how smoothly this book went together. The enthusiasm which was extended towards myself and this project in general has given me the ability to take this book's beginning ideas all the way to a published volume. I'd like to especially thank the following people for going the "extra mile" and contributing their special talents towards this book on North American porcelain enamel advertising.

To Peter Schiffer my publisher, and Ian Robertson, my editor, my sincere appreciation for your support and understanding when your telephone rang late at night. I'll limit future calls to no later than midnight!

To Donna Salzman, for taking me on a 22 hour California adventue to photograph signs.

Special thanks to Vivian McLaughlin, Director of The Resource and Research Center for Beaver Falls, Pennsylvania, for assistance with the Ingram-Richardson historical information.

To Sharon Callender for her professional assistance with text layout and last minute additions.

And finally to all my contributors. It was so rewarding to meet with you and photograph your collections. My heartfelt thanks to each of you. it's you that made this book a reality.

Mike Bruner

Revised price guide: 1999
Copyright © 1999 by Michael Bruner
Library of Congress Catalog Card Number: 99-60439

ISBN: 0-7643-0816-5
Printed in China
1 2 3 4

Published by Schiffer Publishing Ltd.
4880 Lower Valley Road
Atglen, PA 19310
Phone: (610) 593-1777; Fax: (610) 593-2002
E-mail: Schifferbk@aol.com
Please visit our web site catalog at **www.schifferbooks.com**

In Europe, Schiffer books are distributed by Bushwood Books
6 Marksbury Avenue Kew Gardens
Surrey TW9 4JF England
Phone: 44 (0)181 392-8585; Fax: 44 (0)181 392-9876
E-mail: Bushwd@aol.com

This book may be purchased from the publisher.
Include $3.95 for shipping. Please try your bookstore first.
We are interested in hearing from authors with book ideas on related subjects.
You may write for a free printed catalog.

CONTRIBUTORS

The following is an alphabetical listing of contributors that have shared their time and allowed me to photograph items for the book. Some individuals wish to remain anonymous, and their contributions are much appreciated.

Bob Alexander, Winter Haven, Florida
Archer Classic Cars, Duluth, Minnesota
Barry Baker, Chicago, Illinois
Dave Beck, Mediapolis, Iowa
Jim Bergman, Anchorage, Alaska
John Bobroff, Running Springs, California
Larry Burch, Palestine, Texas
Robert Carty, San Diego, California
Rody Cummings, Blackfoot, Idaho
Alan Drew, Colonia, New Jersey
Mervin Eisel, Fort Ripley, Minnesota
Frank Feher, West Sacramento, California
Bill Fraser, Cumming, Georgia
Ken Fritz, Parkside Antique Mall, Princeton, Wisconsin
Scott Given, Lodi, Ohio
Mick Hoover, Mackay, Idaho
Bob Knudsen Jr., American Falls, Idaho
Kim and Mary Kokles, Dallas, Texas
Rod Krupka, Ortonville, Michigan
Dave Lane, Tulsa, Oklahoma
Robert Lloyd, Windsor, Ontario, Canada
Dave Lowenthal, Canyon Country, California
Fred Lupton, Dearborn, Michigan
Doug MacGillvary, Manchester, Connecticut
Gary Metz, Roanoke, Virginia
Dave Monahan, Warwick, Rhode Island
Bernie Nagel, White Lake Township, Michigan
Jim Oswald, Centerville, Utah
Railroad Memories Museum, Spooner, Wisconsin
Roy Reed, Fontana, California
Dan Reynolds, Owensboro, Kentucky
Larry Schrof, Geneseo, Illinois
Jack Tanner, White City, Florida
Ted Tear, Marshall, Michigan
Johnny C. Venison, Reno, Nevada
Viking Antiques, Manitowoc, Wisconsin
Tom and Sherry Watt, Glyndon, Minnesota
Ben J. Weaver, Warsaw, Indiana
Dennis Weber, Saint Joseph, Missouri
Larry and Nancy Werner, Winfield, Illinois
Wendell White, Bountiful, Utah

CONTENTS

PREFACE

The past few years have seen a tremendous growth in collecting antique advertising. Of the many media used by companies to bring attention to their products or services, none seem to have had the overall appeal of porcelain enamel. The process of creating porcelain signs is actually an art in itself, and the influx of new collectors in the market place attests to porcelain enamel advertising's beauty. Few collectibles are made with such long-lasting properties or have been found in such diversity as porcelain enamel advertising.

For all the magnificent designs that have turned up through the years, it is interesting to note that the hobby of collecting this advertising is of relatively recent vintage. Possibly collectors couldn't see the forest for the trees! So many times we have been bombarded with advertising in our everyday life that we really paid little attention to such matter-of-fact items. I've been to many places that had some type of porcelain sign outside the building, only to find out the owner had no idea that the advertising sign I mentioned was on the premises!

Like so many other collectibles, the stimulus for collecting porcelain enamel advertising was that it is no longer being manufactured, and it is gradually disappearing from the eye of the general public. The past few years have seen the removal of most of the remaining porcelain enamel signs that were still "in use." Normally, a long search will not turn up anything but the most common pieces still doing service. With little porcelain advertising to be found in its original place, those wanting a piece of the action must now turn to the collector's market to build a collection.

The heartbeat of any hobby is the ability to buy, sell or trade. Collecting porcelain advertising is certainly no different in that it's the people in the hobby that make it an enjoyable experience. It is possible to build a fine collection by staying at home, writing letters, making phone calls, et cetera. However, to really network yourself, it pays to get out to shows. Many dealers are specialists in advertising, and come up with some pretty unusual items. A few shows throughout the country even specialize in advertising, and a good mix of porcelain advertising usually will be present. These shows are generally well advertised in the major antique publications. Don't get discouraged by the fact that some of the pieces you want for you collection are not available. Patience will almost always pay off in the long run. And as far as prices go, if you like it and you can afford it, then buy it! I've been involved in several hobbies through the years, and in my judgment collecting porcelain advertising will "go through the roof" in a few years. Not every sign will be a breadwinner, but on the average most advertising does appreciate in value over time. This is especially true on the better items.

As you go through this book, you can't help but notice the tremendous degree of diversity that can be found in porcelain advertising. Not only signs, but dozens of other everyday items were made with a porcelain message. Keep in mind that you are looking only at the "tip of the iceberg." There were thousands of porcelain signs manufactured in this country during the last hundred years. However, due to World War II's scrap effort, possibly as few as 30 percent of the total signs manufactured have survived. Despite this seemingly discouraging view, there are endless possibilities for new finds in basements, attics, bulk plants, and defunct manufacturing facilities. Proof of this can be seen at antique advertising shows, with a never-ending stream of new discoveries coming through the door.

This volume will give you an idea of the beauty and diverse graphics that can be found in this very collectible are of Americana.

I look forward to hearing from you. Please feel free to write me c/o 4103 Lotus Drive, Waterford, MI 48329.

Mike Bruner

INTRODUCTION

To help us understand how porcelain enamel advertising came into collectible status, a brief understanding of its day-to-day use is helpful. As the art of porcelain enamel production was perfected, it became an inexpensive way for a business to promote its products. By the turn of the century porcelain enamel advertising became so commonplace that few merchants could be found without some type of porcelain sign being displayed. No longer was porcelain advertising a luxury. It became the standard by which to judge all other advertising forms.

As the years progressed, so did the imaginations of those responsible for creating the signs. Square and rectangular signs gave way to extravagant "die-cut" designs. New effort was put into the color schemes. Anything and everything was tried on porcelain enamel. This kept manufacturers busy for the better part of the century.

In time, though, many manufacturers went by the wayside. The smaller concerns could not compete. The rising costs involved in the production of porcelain enamel made many businesses consider alternative methods of advertising. This spelled doom for the sign manufacturers. By the 1970s, the production of porcelain enamel advertising became a closed chapter in American history.

The good news is that collectors have recognized porcelain enamel as a historical connection to the past. It is a link to the products and services that made this country great. Unfortunately, some of the companies that advertised in porcelain are no longer with us, but many are still around, possibly due to the porcelain advertising they used throughout the years.

The products to be found advertised in porcelain are almost endless. As you read through the book, you will see the wide range of advertisers who used this medium. There seem to be certain subjects that received more of the advertising market than others, particularly the products or services that were frequently used by the public. Leading the list would be petroleum signs,

and any advertising relating to the automobile or gasoline. It would be safe to say that more petroleum-related porcelain enamel advertising was produced that there was in any other category. Many collectors specialize in "petro" advertising and find the number of items produced over the years nearly endless. Other companies that made heavy use of porcelain advertising are manufacturers of beer, paints and varnishes, telephone, tobacco, and soda pop.

As a collector, don't make the mistake of trying to acquire everything. If you want to collect by the pound, that is fine; but keep in mind how much is out there! It's just not practical to think that you can collect everything that was produced. Instead, set your sights on a more realistic approach. One of the most common would be to specialize in a certain company or product. One collector I know collects only blue and white porcelain, and he says it goes great with his graniteware! Possibly a special interest in your personal life will find its way to your collection. As an example, I know several people who are telephone company employees that specialize in porcelain telephone advertising. After a brief period you'll find out what it is that interests you.

You'll find this book divided into several chapters. Each chapter covers items by manufacturing design, rather than subject matter. The only exception to this is chapter five, which features gasoline pump signs. Each photograph will have a brief description plus any relevant comments. This will be followed by the item's measurements—width first, then height. The approximate age of the sign will also be given. Please keep in mind that estimating the age of a sign is done by using a combination of several techniques. These are covered in a separate section in the book.

For those of you privileged enough to have lived in the era of porcelain advertising, get ready for a trip down memory lane. And for those of us that wish to go back to a time we never saw, the following pages will provide a vivid portrait of our past in porcelain enamel advertising.

ESTIMATING A SIGN'S AGE

Very few porcelain signs have been made with the date of manufacture, or intended use on them. The most notable exception to this would be Coca-Cola signs that had their manufacturing date ink-stamped on them. Most of these date to the 1930s. Some automobile signs have been found with the year of their service on them as well. For the most part, a sign's age cannot be pinpointed without a date right on the sign. There are, however, some techniques that can be helpful in determining the approximate age of a sign.

The most scholastic method requires that the name of the manufacturer to be on the sign. If this information is known, then some research can tell you the dates during which the company was in business. This may not in itself accomplish much, because many companies were producing signs for decades. If the street address of the manufacturer is on the sign you might get a better idea of a sign's age, because many times a company's operations at a particular address were for only a brief time. These methods take some real knowledge of the companies that were in business, and you might spend considerable time researching this information.

Another approach would be to "size up" the product advertised. This means that if you know the history of the product or service that is advertised on the sign, you can use this information to help you determine the sign's age.

As an example, if you found a "Mobilgas" sign with the "pegasus" logo on it, you would know that the sign was later than the 1920s. Mobil did not use the pegasus logo until the 1930s. Similarly, if you guessed that a Brazil Beer sign dates in the 1940s, you would be considerably off, as this company was doing business during the first years of the century.

Although these methods are helpful, using them required a knowledge of the products being advertised. There is another method that seems to work even better.

The most accepted and reliable method of dating a sign is the look and feel of the porcelain. Most of the older signs—those dating before 1930—were made using a stencil. This technique always produced a "bumpy" feel at the edges where different colors meet. Called "shelving," it was caused by the firing of more than one coat of porcelain. Some signs were fired five or six times, leaving the effect of shelving quite pronounced. Normally a sign made after 1940 will not have a high degree of this layered feel.

As unusual as this may seem, the back side of a sign may tell you more than the front. A porcelain coat will normally be found on the back side. The color of this coating can range from a light gray to a bluish-black and everything in between. The oldest signs will have many small "spots" where there is no porcelain. Some signs may have over a hundred of these small spots. This would indicate a sign of pre-1930 vintage, as manufacturers used methods that eliminated most of these spots after that time. This technique is for signs with the advertising only on one side.

A high degree of hand production work is evident on older signs. It's common to find fingerprints fired right into the porcelain, sometimes in two or more colors! Once in a while you will find a set of numbers finger-written and fired into the porcelain. Let's say, as an example, that you find the number "3-07." You could assume that the sign in your hands was manufactured in March of 1907!

As you gain experience as a collector, you will find your abilities for estimating a sign's age have improved. Talking with other collectors is helpful. You can learn much, quickly, from their knowledge.

GRADING CONDITION

The increased use of the mail and the telephone for buying and selling antique advertising has created a need to develop a standard grading scale. Condition on a piece is of extreme importance when buying a sign "sight unseen." In the past there have been some problems in grading. By using the photographs in this book, hopefully these problems will be minimized.

In describing a sign the seller must make and accurate assessment of damage. The buyer expects to have no surprises when the sign arrives, and if it has been graded correctly the buyer will be inclined to follow through with the transaction.

The majority of signs in "collectible" condition will fall into the grading scale between a rating of six and ten. Those pieces that are below grade 6.0 have lost enough of their eye appeal to be of limited interest. To help give a better idea of the number that would match condition, more than one photograph is shown for the conditions of seven, eight and nine. To get a more accurate guide to condition a value can be expressed in decimal points. As an example, to grade a sign between an eight and nine we would grade it an 8.5. This universally accepted system of grading offers better understanding than using terms such as mint, near mint, very good, good, et cetera.

The following descriptions, in conjunction with the photo references below, should help you grade porcelain enamel signs.

Grade 10: Like new, out-of-the-box condition. Eyelets, if any, can show use or be missing, but no chips can be around the eyelet holes.

Grade 9.5: Very close to like-new condition with original luster to the porcelain but with a slight amount of damage, such as small screw hole chips, light scratches or a small chip to non-critical sections of the image area. Small edge nicks in limited numbers could be found.

Grade 9.0: Small areas of edge damage that do not detract from the overall appearance of the advertising. Several small or one larger edge chip are acceptable. Porcelain gloss should be intact, but the surface may show slight signs of use. The image area may have a small chip.

Grade 8.5: Chips become more numerous or may go into some of the image area. There may be slight loss of luster to part of the porcelain. Edge damage becomes more prominent, but does not detract from the overall appearance.

Grade 8.0: The image area may have a small amount of damage that will detract somewhat, but this will be confined to a minimum. There can be surface scratches or loss of luster. Damage outside the image area is more pronounced, with many edge chips or larger size chips to the screw holes or the flange area.

Grade 7.5: More noticeable damage to the sign with several larger size chips. The porcelain may have loss of luster in some areas and surface scratches could detract somewhat. Chips in the image area will be present, but will not be so large that a significant amount of eye-appeal is lost. Flange damage could be extensive.

Grade 7.0: Chipping is more pronounced, with many edge chips and several chips in the image area. There may be chips in a critical area of the image. Much wear could be present with significant loss of porcelain luster and scratches.

Grade 6.0: There is significant loss of eye-appeal, with the image area damaged considerably. Several larger size chips will be present, and flange damage could be severe.

Keep in mind that on flanged signs and signs that have an image area on both sides, a grade must be established for each side. Manufacturer's defects will occasionally be present and although they are not considered damage, they should be mentioned.

The following chart will give an idea as to how to properly grade condition. The left column gives a condition rating; the right column shows where to look for a photo of a sign in this condition. For convenience all photos are found in chapter one.

GRADE	PHOTO
10	Page 18 top right
9.5	Page 20 bottom left
9.5	Page 20 top left
9.0	Page 66 bottom right
9.0	Page 22 center
8.5	Page 62 bottom left
8.5	Page 27 bottom left
8.0	Page 83 center
8.0	Page 26 left
7.5	Page 16 top
7.5	Page 37 bottom
7.0	Page 23 top
7.0	Page 13 center right
6.0	Page 50 center

As a rule, all chips are not created equal! Edge chips are not as significant as the same size chips on the inside are. Normally the edge area can expect to have some damage, and this is not as critical as the center being damaged. The principal question to answer is how much the damage detracts from the appeal of the sign. A 30" Conoco minuteman sign in super condition, except that a chip the size of a quarter "took out" the minuteman's face, will go from a condition of 9.5 plus to around 7.0, simply because few collectors would find a faceless minutemen very attractive. This is especially true at the prices these signs are going for!

If a sign is two-sided, then a grade must be given for each side. If the sign has a flange, a mention of the condition should be made, keeping in mind that flange damage is not as critical to a sign's appeal as damage to the face.

As many collectors "network" themselves with others that share similar interests, it will pay to be as honest and accurate as possible in grading the condition of signs.

REPAIRED SIGNS

As prices continue to increase in the market, repairing a sign seems to make good sense. There are times, however, when repairing can be an exercise in futility. The basis for all sign repairs is how the sign will look compared to its appearance before the work was done. The decision is up to the owner. You must ask whether the damage is so unsightly that it's going to make the repair a worthwhile investment. If the answer is no, then it is best to just leave the sign the way it is. If you decide to have repairs made, the next step is to get the job done right.

There are several levels of quality in the sign repair business. "So-so" and "terrible" are the levels most frequently encountered. Unfortunately, most of the sign repairs out there never reach the quality of "great," due to the amateur nature of the work. Anyone can get out a can of body filler and "go to town." However, to do professional work requires much practice, and work of truly high quality comes from only a select few craftspeople.

When a sign that was damaged enough to be rated a seven is repaired so that it appears to be a mint condition sign, then you have a quality repair. There are people that can do repairs of this level, but they are expensive and you may not want to make the investment unless it will enhance the sign's value.

If you have a sign that has a market value of $300 in mint condition and the repair costs are $275, it might be in your best interest to leave it and invest in a more worthwhile repair. Normally, the higher-priced signs will be worth the cost of repairs—again, provided the workmanship is high caliber.

How does a repair affect the value of a sign? There are some variables to consider, including the extent of repair on the sign and the quality of the work. On average, though, a sign that had a quality repair job would be worth at least 60–75 percent of what the sign would have been worth in mint condition with no repairs. As an example, if a given sign has a market value in mint condition of $1,000, then a sign repaired so that it appears to be in mint condition should be worth at least $650 to $750. Again, it must be emphasized that these figures are for quality repairs only. Home-type "garage" repairs most likely will do little to enhance a sign's value, and may even lower it!

In conclusion, the decision to repair a sign is solely that of the sign's owner. However, dealers and collectors selling repaired signs have an ethical responsibility to be up-front and honest about repairs. Having available a photo of the pre-repaired sign has been suggested by numerous collectors.

Chapter One

FLAT ONE-SIDED SIGNS

The signs in this chapter were all manufactured with the advertising on one side only. You will notice that the placement of mounting holes changes from one sign to the next. Each design called for a different support method. Most of the signs seen here will be for mounting to a wall. Some could be used in other situations such as fastening to a cart, or a cooler. Others were designed to be mounted on the sides of trucks. A few were made to fasten together with another of the same sign, back to back.

The California Motor Service Association used these small two-color signs for their members. No doubt they were intended for use at garages and service stations. These date from the 1920s. *Courtesy of John Romagnoli.* $300.

Sunkist Grower four-color "self framed" sign. The light green border is slightly raised and has a finished edge around the sign. Dates from the 1950s. Measures 9 1/2" x 14". *Courtesy of John Bobroff.* $200

Allied Automotive Industries of California LTD. Measures 15" x 18" and dates from around 1950. *Courtesy of Frank Feher.* $300

Feen-a-mint four-color sign. This design is quite a bit more detailed than later versions. Dates around the 1920s. 30" x 8". *Courtesy of Dan Reynolds.* $1200

Beech-Nut Chewing Tobacco. This sign is from the 1930s and is not easy to find in such superb condition. Measures 22" x 10 1/2". *Author's collection.* $400

Hudson Valley Coke. Measures 35" x 14". Manufactured by L.D. Nelke Signs —New York, and dates around 1930. *Courtesy of John Bobroff.* $300

Here's an outstanding example of the artistry involved in the manufacture of porcelain enamel. Although no advertising appears directly on the piece, it possibly was made for Poll-Parrot Shoes as part of a larger display. It measures 14" x 35", and seems to date from around 1930. *Author's collection.* $700

Large Coca-Cola self-framed sign. These were intended as outdoor display signs, but you would never know it from the condition of this one. This example measures 4' x 8' and was manufactured by Penn. Enamel, New Castle, Pennsylvania. As with many Coca-Cola signs, the date has been ink-stamped on the sign, in this case 1932. *Courtesy of Ted Tear.* $3000

Golden Shell Motor Oil die-cut sign. The Shell logo went through several slight modifications over the years. The one shown here dates it to around 1930. Measures 12" x 12". *Courtesy of Bob Knudsen Jr.* $1300

Railway Express Agency "diamond" sign. These were produced by the thousands, but despite these copious quantities, high demand has kept their value relatively high. Measures 11" x 11". Dates in the 1930s. *Author's collection.* $100

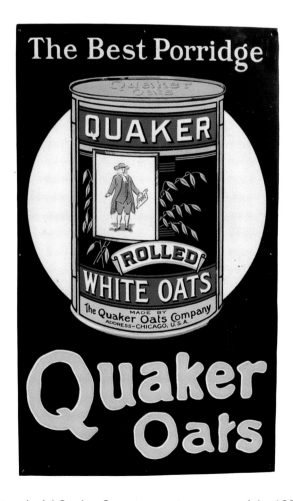

For country store advertising collectors, it just doesn't get any better than this! The beautiful Crisco die-cut sign pictured here was in service around 1910. It measures 14" x 20". Ink-stamped at the bottom right "B.S. CO. 166 N. STATE ST. CHI. & BALTO ENL & NOV CO., MD." *Author's Collection.* $3500.

This colorful Quaker Oats sign was in use around the 1890s! It measures 18" x 30". *Private Collection.* $3500.

J.T. BOWENS
LICENSED HAWKER
BOSTON.

J.T. Bowens—Licensed Hawker. Definitely unusual! Very thick crude porcelain. Measures 26" x 12". This should date to around the turn of the century. *Courtesy of John Bobroff.* $250

These were used by Flying-A gas stations in the 1940s-50s. Despite their simplicity, the manufacturer (unknown) managed to use five colors of porcelain. Measures 8" x 11". *Courtesy of Bob Knudsen Jr.* $350

This great looking Old Dutch Cleanser sign dates around 1915. It measures 14" x 20". Ink-stamped at the bottom "B.S. CO. 166 N. STATE ST. CHI. & BEAVER FALLS, PA." *Author's collection.* $1200

The R.G. Sullivan's Cigar sign was manufactured in two similar styles. Upon close examination, you can notice the rough edges around the letters on the sign photographed here. This sign was also manufactured in a much "cleaner" version, with the lettering having sharp, well-defined edges. Measures 23" x 10 1/2". These date to the 1930s. *Author's collection.* $350

Sunshine Biscuits. This dates from around 1910. Notice the corner holes are outside the logo. Measures 12" x 12". *Courtesy of John Bobroff.* $250

OK Portland Cement. Dates around the 1920s. Measures 20" x 30". *Courtesy of John Bobroff.* $300

Spearhead Chewing Tobacco. Measures 14" x 6", and dates in the 1930s. *Author's collection.* $250

Gulf States Telephone strip sign. One-of-a-kind. This dates around the 1920s. Measures 18" x 3". *Courtesy of Frank Feher.* $1000

Tide Water was an early gasoline supplier. This two-color sign measures approximately 28" x 8" and dates to around 1920. *Courtesy of John Bobroff.* $300.

Pittston Gazette. Measures 16" x 8", and dates around 1915. This one is by ING-RICH, Beaver Falls, PA. *Courtesy of Dan Reynolds.* $250

Canadian National Express. This has a half-inch of turned-down metal going around the sign. It could be mounted on a wood "square" that was the size of the sign. Made in Canada by P & M, Orilla, Ontario. Measures 16" x 16". *Author's collection.* $850

Murphy Paints. Paint companies put a lot of color on many of their signs, the one pictured being no exception with at least seven colors! Measures approximately 36" x 24". From a building in St. Joseph, Missouri. $500

Mobiloil Certified Service. This sign uses a design similar to the "fried egg" style that was used by Atlantic Refining. A few of these were found in a warehouse recently, but not enough to meet the desires of the petro collectors market. Measures 19 1/2" x 19 1/2", and dates around the 1930s. *Courtesy of Mick Hoover.* $850

This beautiful Grand Union Hotel sign features the superb graphics of a late 19th century work of art. It was no doubt placed in conspicuous locations throughout New York City and today remains as a testimonial of the splendor found in that era. It measures approximately 7" x 4". *Courtesy of Pete Keim.* $350.

Monitor Stoves and Ranges. Edge damage does little to detract from the eye-catching design. Notice the great early battleship *Monitor* is done in lithograph. There is also an eagle near the bottom done by the same process. This sign should date to 1910 or earlier. Measures 18" x 15". *Courtesy of John Bobroff.* $500

Beauty Shoppe. Measures 18" x 9". There are several similar variations of this sign. Dates from around the 1920s. *Author's collection.* $450

Coca-Cola Fountain Service. A great looking example! Measures 27" x 14". Ink-stamped "TENN EN MFG Co. NASHVILLE, MADE IN USA." *Courtesy of Dan Reynolds.* $1400

Sinclair Oils. These were used on oil carts. The larger one measures 12" in diameter. The small one 6". Both are scarce. petro collectors refer to this design as Sinclair's "bar logo." These date to around 1940. *Courtesy of Wendell White.* $700 ea.

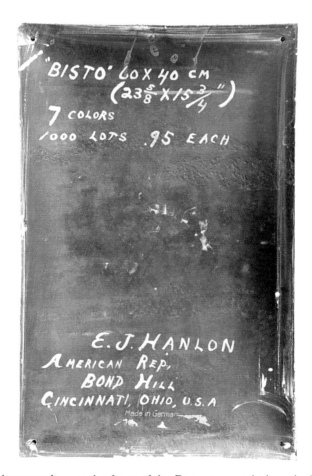

Outstanding graphics abound in this colorful Bisto convex sign. The convex shape gives a hinting of the sign's German manufacture. It was produced by Boos 7 Hahn, Ortenberg-Baden, and measures 16" x 24". It dates to around 1930. *Private Collection.* $3000.

As appealing as the front of the Bisto sign might be, it's the back on this on that commands attention. Of interest is the production figure of 1000 lots. Even more intriguing is the fact that they were sold at 95¢ each! Possibly this piece was a sample sent over for approval, as it's unlikely that such technical information would be on the back of an entire shipment. *Private Collection.*

17

The exact use of this Riche Coal Co. sign is uncertain. However, it may have been found on stoker units used in early home heating systems. It measures approximately 5" x 3". *Courtesy of John Bobroff.* $125.

Mayo's Plug. The central image on these were done by the lithograph process. Measures 6 1/2" x 13". These date to the 1920 era. *Courtesy of Dan Reynolds.* $800

Beacon Ethyl Gasoline. What a sign! It would be difficult to come up with a more eye-catching logo. These date to around the 1930s when "ethyl" gasoline was just getting started. It measures 30" x 48". *Courtesy of Bob Knudsen Jr.* $2200

Bell System Stop Accidents "hubcap" sign. Measures 6 inches in diameter. These were placed on the back of lineman's trucks to indicate the crew was safety conscious. These also were found with small rectangular signs that had the year on them, to be placed below this sign. These date to around 1930. *Author's collection.* $350

Quaker Maid Milk. Measures 41" x 24", and dates in the 1960 era. Ink-stamped at the bottom "CAMEO GILA." *Courtesy of John Bobroff.* $400

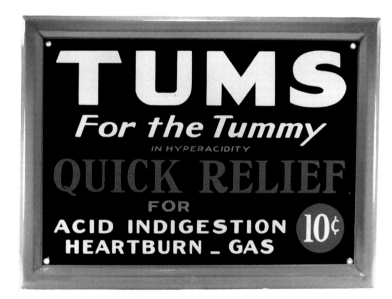

Tums five-color self-framed sign. Measures 24" x 17". Dates to around the 1930s. *Author's Collection.* $900.

Jersey Central Lines. Measures 18" round. These were used mostly on bridge overpasses. Dates from the 1940s. *Courtesy of John Bobroff.* $300

This convex Bond Bread sign was produced in Germany around 1930. It was manufactured as a salesman's sample. Marked at the bottom "PYRO-EMAIL." Measures 19" x 13". *Courtesy of Dave and Beth Justice.*

Climax Plug Tobacco. Measures 14" x 15". Dates back to around 1900. *Courtesy of John Bobroff.* $200

Sinclair Opaline Motor oils. Measures 11" x 17". The "vertical bar" design dates it to the 1920s. *Courtesy of Wendell White.* $700

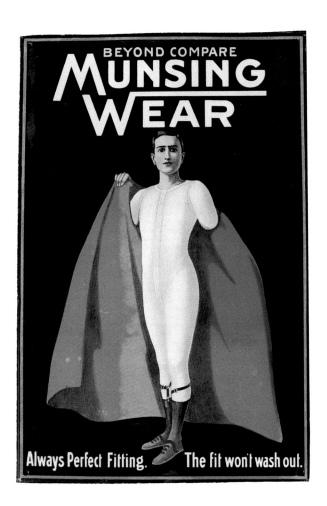

Fire Insurance Company of Canada. Many beautiful signs were produced through the years in Canada. The large beaver at the top certainly adds to its eye appeal! Measures 12" x 18". This sign should date to the 1930s. *Courtesy of Bob Knudsen Jr.* $350

Few porcelain signs can rival the exceptional graphics found on this early Munsing Wear framed-edge sign. This 24" x 36" beauty was manufactured in Germany by Robert Dold of Offenburg around 1900. *Private Collection.* $7000

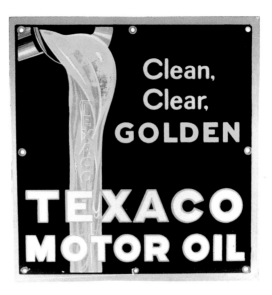

Texaco Motor Oil. Measures 15 1/2" x 16". This is a great-looking example. Many of these had a tendency to fade out in the yellow area from being exposed to the elements. Dates around the 1930s. *Courtesy of Mick Hoover.* $800

Few graphics are more appealing than those using an American Indian on a logo. Five Roses Flour had a winner with this 26" x 42" wall-mount sign. Dates to the 1920s. *Private Collection.* $3500.

Ojaco Paints. Measures 17" x 20". Large paint cans were frequently part of a paint manufacturer's logo. This one dates in the 1930s. *Courtesy of John Bobroff.* $250

Florida Power & Light Company oval sign. These were mostly used on fences at sub-stations. Measures 16 1/2" x 11", and dates in the 1950s. *Courtesy of Scott Given.* $200

Drink Dr. Pepper. This dates around 1940 and can also be found in a self-framed style with a green border. Measures 24" x 10". Ink stamped "McMATH AXILROD—DALLAS." *Author's collection.* $500

Sinclair Opaline Authorized Dealer. Dates in the 1920s. Measures 48" x 20". *Courtesy of John Bobroff.* 600

NevrNox Gasoline caught the motorist's eye with its three-color diamond-pattern sign. It measures approximately 30" x 20" and dates from the 1930s. *Courtesy of John Bobroff.* $600.

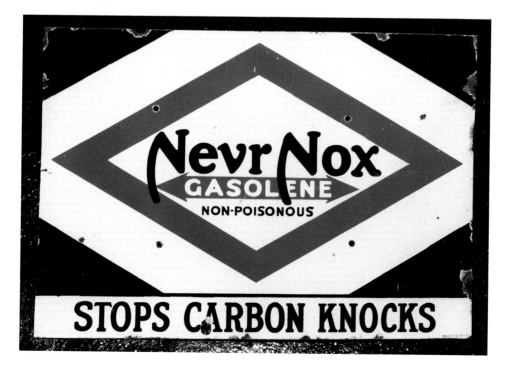

Key System. These were a part of an inter-urban transportation system in California. This is from the 1930s era and measures 22" x 17". *Courtesy of John Bobroff.* $200

This "Fire" sign was placed on a wall next to a telephone. It measures 10" x 7", and has thick old porcelain. No doubt from the 1920s era. *Courtesy of John Bobroff.* $125

The Washington Water Power Co. Not all power company signs were created equal! The use of "Reddy Kilowatt" in the logo enhances this sign's value considerably. Measures 12" x 12", and dates from the 1950s. *Courtesy of Scott Given.* $150

Sometimes simple is better, as is the case on this Beachs World Soap sign from the era around 1915. It measures approximately 16" x 7". *Courtesy of Pete Keim.* $150.

Dawn Patrol Alarm signs were used on the front of alarm boxes. Measures 12" x 10". Dates in the 1940s. *Courtesy of Mick Hoover.* $150

Good Luck Service used this die-cut oval sign in the 1950s. It measures approximately 20" x 12". *Courtesy of John Bobroff.* $300.

Star Tobacco. This is a great-looking old piece dating from the 1920s era. These are fairly common in "rough" condition, but are scarce to find like the example shown here. Thick old porcelain and the "plug" of tobacco was done by using a lithograph process. *Author's collection.* $450

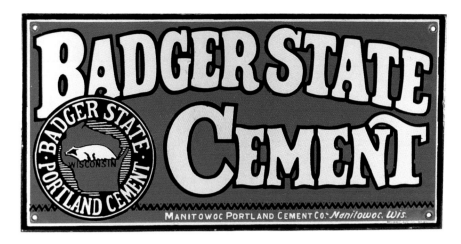

Badger State Cement. Measures 18" x 9". Ink stamped at the bottom "RELIANCE ADVERTISING COMPANY—NEW YORK." Dates from around 1930. *Author's collection.* $850

The Orange County sign is from California. It incorporates the "independent" telephone logo. Dates from the era around 1910 and is the only example known. Measures 15" x 15". *Author's collection.* $1700

American Bosch. Measures 16" x 24", and dates around 1930. Ink stamped "MADE IN USA." *Courtesy of Bob Knudsen Jr.* $700

American Express Travelers Cheques sign. Measures 10" x 4 1/2", and dates around the 1930s. *Courtesy of Frank Feher.* $275

The beautiful die-cut "Coca-Cola" sign pictured here was designed to be fastened to the side of a cooler. It measures 18" x 5 1/2", and dates in the 1930s era. *Courtesy of Dan Reynolds.* $950

The Franklin Protective Assn. sign was mounted to a building as a warning to thieves. Measures 8" x 4", and is from the 1920s era. *Courtesy of John Bobroff.* $100

Large "Singer Sewing Machines" wall mount sign. Over the years Singer used several slight variations in this style sign. The best way to spot them is to look at the face of the woman at the machine. Measures 24" x 36", and dates around the 1930s. Stamped "F. FRANCIS AND SONS LTD. LONDON S.E." at the bottom. *Courtesy of John Bobroff.* $700

Jiffy-Namel sign. Measures 16" x 14". Dates in the 1930s. *Courtesy of Bob Alexander.* $200

The Atlantic Refining Co. sign dates from the 1920s. It measures 30" x 20". *Courtesy of Frank Feher.* $500

The Alpha Portland Cement sign was no doubt used on the sides of trucks. It measures 13" in diameter, and dates around the 1920s. Although no manufacturer's stamping appears on the sign, a like-new Ingram-Richardson decal is on the back side. *Author's collection.* $500

Nicolene Motor Oil sign. Measures 36" x 23 1/2", and dates in the 1930s. Notice the arrow on the word "sell" that is pointing to Nicolene logo. *Courtesy of John Bobroff.* $700

Carter's Overalls. These date to the 1920s. Measures 15" x 6". *Courtesy of John Bobroff.* $450

Champion Spark Plugs self-framed sign. The large spark plug really makes this sign *eye catching! Measures 30" x 14", and dates around the 1930s. Stamped "MADE IN USA" at bottom. Courtesy of Bob Knudsen Jr.* $950

Wisconsin Creameries used this heavy gauge Ice Cream sign around the 1930s. It measures 18" x 12". *Author's collection.* $400

These two round railroad signs were used in the 1920s and 1930s.
Courtesy of John Bobroff. $1600.

This little Sweet Heart Products could have been used as a small door push. It measures only 5" x 5". Dates around the 1920s. *Courtesy of Bernie Nagel.* $125

This California State Auto Association sign was placed at roadside locations. It measures 28" x 23", and dates around the 1920s era. Notice the old "AAA" logo at the bottom. *Courtesy of Frank Feher.* $375

Old Dutch Cleanser is features on this strip sign dating from the 1920s. It measures approximately 4" x 26". *Courtesy of Pete Keim.* $150.

Wooley Coal Co. sign. No doubt "Maplewood" was the name of the town where they were located. Measures 14" x 14". From the 1930s. *Courtesy of John Bobroff.* $350

The U.S. Official sign was placed on the outside of a car door window. It has a special bracket on the back for this purpose. Shades of "Elliott Ness"! Measures 17" x 20". You won't be far off guessing the date at 1925. Stamped "BALTIMORE ENAMEL 200 FIFTH AVE N.Y." *Courtesy of Mick Hoover.* $800

Seilheimer's Ginger Ale signs were found en masse a few years ago. Despite this fact, they seem to have all disappeared into the collector's marketplace. They all had a wooden backboard-type frame and have heavy porcelain. The sign measures 18" x 10", and dates around 1930. Marked "L.D. NELKE SIGNS N.Y." at the bottom. *Author's collection.* $200

Monarch paint strip sign. Measures 32" x 4". Dates around 1920. *Author's collection.* $450

This sign was used by "White Rose" service stations and features their logo. It measures 17 1/2" x 18", and dates around the 1940s. *Courtesy of Bob Knudsen Jr.* $400

Blue Coal. Dates around the 1940s, and measures 10" x 10". *Courtesy of Rod Krupka.* $100

Oshkosh B'Gosh Overalls. Uncle Sam helped this one out quite a bit! Measures 30" x 10", and dates around the 1920s. Stamped at the bottom right "BURDICK, CONSUMERS BLDG. CHI. & BEAVER FALLS, PA." *Courtesy of John Bobroff.* $600

Telephone Pay Station sign from the Lincoln Telephone and Telegraph Company. The two logos were done by the lithographic process. Only a couple of these are known to exist. Measures 24" x 5", and dates around 1920. *Author's collection.* $2300

Tampa Nugget 5¢ Cigars. Measures 24" x 7", and dates around the 1940s. *Courtesy of Dan Reynolds.* $250

No Smoking sign from Texaco. Only a few of these are known. It dates from the 1920s, and measures 24" x 6". *Author's collection.* $1900

The Union Ice Company. This would date to around 1940. It measures 17" x 17". *Courtesy of John Bobroff.* $350

Canby's apparently was a department store this oval sign graphically puts their image on porcelain. It dates from the 1940s and measures approximately 28" x 18". *Courtesy of John Bobroff.* $200.

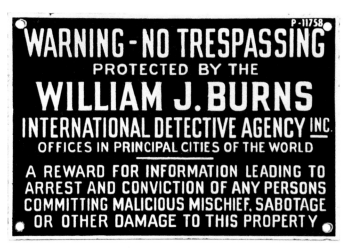

William J. Burns warning sign. Measures 9" x 6", and dates in the 1930s. *Courtesy of Mick Hoover.* $75

Union 76 Certified Car Condition Service sign. Measures 22" in diameter. Dates from the 1950s era. *Courtesy of Wendell White.* $350

Mobiloil Authorized Service sign. Measures 19 1/2" x 24". These date to around the 1930s. *Courtesy of Bob Knudsen Jr.* $450

"Steamro" Red Hots strip sign. Measures 17 1/2" x 22", and is from around the 1930s era. *Courtesy of Bernie Nagel.* $175

The Cyclone Fence sign pictured here is one of the few porcelain signs that are still in service. This one has the words "Los Angeles" in large letters. Measures 13 1/2" x 4". These date to the 1950s. *Courtesy of Rod Krupka.* $40

Mother Penn die-cut sign. These date from the 1930s. Measures 20" x 13", and is marked "RELIANCE ADV. CO. CHICAGO" at the bottom right. *Courtesy of John Bobroff.* $600

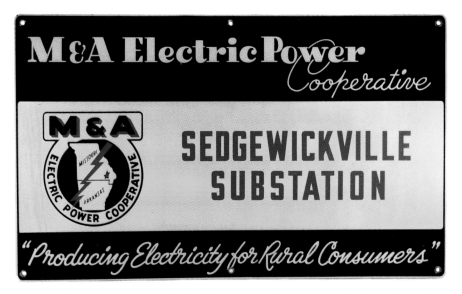

M & A Electric Power sign. Each of these were "custom" made for the location served. Measures 30" x 18". From the 1950s. *Courtesy of Dennis Weber.* $150

Drink Coca-Cola sign. It measures 35" x 10", and would date to the late 1920s. Marked at the bottom "BALTIMORE ENAMEL 200 5TH AVE N.Y. MADE IN U.S.A. COPYRIGHT 1925." *Courtesy of Dan Reynolds.* $1000

The exact use for this 5¢ sign is uncertain. One thing for sure though, a nickel went a long way when this was in use! Measures 10" x 7 1/2", and dates around 1930. Marked "70-G" at the bottom. *Courtesy of Bob Knudsen Jr.* $100

Lehigh Anthracite die-cut sign. Measures 12" x 12", and dates in the 1930s. *Courtesy of John Bobroff.* $250

Sweet-Orr Overalls. The color in the center graphics was done by the lithographic process. Measures 20" x 14". Dates from around the 1920s. *Courtesy of John Bobroff.* $650

SPITTING
ON STATIONS, PLATFORMS AND APPROACHES
BEING A MISDEMEANOR, IS PUNISHABLE BY
$500 FINE, A YEAR IN PRISON, OR BOTH.
SANITARY CODE SEC. 194
PENAL CODE SEC. 15
BY ORDER
BOARD OF HEALTH

This sign was used by the city of New York in the subways. Despite its crude demeanor, it seems to appeal to many. A quantity of these came on the market several years ago, but have all found homes. Measures 18" x 5". From the 1930s. *Author's collection.* $250

Southeastern Utilities oval sign. Measures 16 1/2" x 11", and dates from the 1950s. *Courtesy of Scott Given.* $200

The California Insurance Company. The bear in the logo really is nice; it is standing on buildings in the downtown district of San Francisco. Measures 18" x 12", and dates around 1915. *Courtesy of Frank Feher.* $1000

Trinity Cement wall sign. These date to the 1930s. Measures 30" x 26". Marked "BURDICK N—AMERICAN BLDG. CHI. & BALTO. ENL. & NOV. CO. MD." *Courtesy of John Bobroff.* $350

BPS strip sign. Measures 24" x 5". Dates in the 1920s. BPS stands for "Best Paint Sold." *Author's collection.* $400

John Deere wall sign with a metal border. Measures 72" x 24". Dates around 1940. Marked "VERTIBRITE SIGNS—CHICAGO" at the bottom. *Courtesy of Dan Reynolds.* $700

Jewelers Security Alliance sign. Measures 7" x 3 1/2". Dates from the 1930s. *Author's collection.* $125

Lehigh Portland Cement. This is quite intricate for a cement logo. It measures 12" x 12", and would date to around the 1930s. *Author's collection.* $250

The three Husky signs pictured here were used at truck stops. They were placed at designated "pet stops." These date to around 1955, and they measure 24" x 12" each. *Courtesy of Wendell White.* $175

Bull's Eye Beer. Measures 18" x 18". Dates around the 1950s. *Courtesy of John Bobroff.* $500

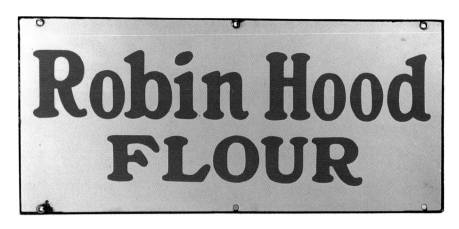

Robin Hood Flower. These are from the 1940s. Measures 20" x 9". *Courtesy of John Bobroff.* $150

Sherwin-Williams Paint used this die-cut sign in the 1930s. It measures approximately 18" x 8". *Courtesy of Tom Licouris.* $600.

This Santa Fe Route sign is one of earliest examples of railroad porcelain advertising to be found. It measures 23" x 14", and dates in before the turn of the century! Marked "B.S. CO. 41 STATE STREET CHICAGO & HARVEY IL." *Courtesy of John Bobroff.* $700

Texaco No Smoking strip sign. Despite the fact that these were produced by the thousands, the collector market seems to be keeping pace. They measure 4" x 23". This one is dated 10-6-53. *Courtesy of Bernie Nagel.* $150

Lehigh Valley Anthracite. Measures 11 1/2" x 9". Dates around the 1950s. *Courtesy of Rod Krupka.* $100

Ward's Vitovim Bread round sign. Measures 27" in diameter, and dates to the 1920s. *Private Collection.* $100.

Feen-A-Mint strip sign. The box put some appeal in an otherwise average looking sign! These date from the 1930s, and measure 29" x 7". *Courtesy of Frank Feher.* $800

This outstanding die-cut Marigold Coach Lines sign dates around 1930. It measures 42" x 11", and is marked "VERIBRITE SIGNS-CHICAGO." *Courtesy of Gary Metz.* $4000

There's no end to the diversity of subject matter available in porcelain advertising as this Toledo Master Painters & Decorators die-cut sign shows! Measures 8" x 10", and dates from around 1930. *Author's collection.* $250

Old Fort Feeds die-cut sign. This measures 40" x 48". It dates in the 1940s. *Courtesy of John Bobroff.* $450

Old Gold self-framed sign. Measures 36" x 12". Dates in the 1930s and is marked at the bottom right "MFG. BY LORRILARD CO. INC." *Courtesy of Dan Reynolds.* $400

Brixment sign. Measures 24" x 18". Dates around the 1930s. *Author's collection.* $300

The Choctaw sign pictured here was fastened to large construction equipment. It measures 10" x 10", and dates in the 1950s. *Courtesy of Bob Knudsen Jr.* $250

This Free Crankcase Service sign by Texaco is another example of the many that were produced over the years for Texaco. It measures 30" x 30", and is from the 1930s. *Courtesy of John Bobroff.* $500

American Express Co. Agency sign. These are difficult to acquire in such outstanding condition. They date back to the turn of the century. Measures 18 1/2" x 16 1/2". Stamped at the bottom "MADE IN ENGLAND" on the left, and in the center "ORME EVANS & CO LTD. 33 BROADWAY", and on the right "4000 MARCH 1902". *Courtesy of Dennis Weber.* $1200

This Local & Long Distance Telephone sign is one of a kind. It measures 24" x 5" and is marked at the bottom "BURDICK CONSUMERS BLDG. CHI. & BALTO ENL. & NOV. CO. MD." It dates around 1920. *Author's collection.* $1200

Copenhagen tobacco strip sign. Most of these were produced on thin metal. Measures 23" x 6", and dates from the 1940s. Stamped at bottom "MADE IN USA." *Courtesy of Dan Reynolds.* $250

"Hot Stuff" was the slogan on this O.H. Little Fuel Co. sign from the 1920s. This company was located in Denver, Colorado. It measures 30" x 9". *Courtesy of John Bobroff.* $200

The Good Humor signs were intended for the sides of ice cream trucks. The one pictured here was found completely painted over with a "local" vendor's brand. Measures 44" x 18". These date to the 1940s. *Courtesy of John Bobroff.* $800

This Longman & Martinez sign is from the turn of the century. It measures 17" x 8", and is marked at the bottom left "MADE IN ENGLAND", and at the bottom right "IMPERIAL ENAMEL CO LTD. 100 WILLIAMS ST. N.Y." *Author's collection.* $300

The Bond Bread sign is usually found with thick base metal and a heavy porcelain glaze. These are from the 1930s, and measure 19" x 14". *Author's collection.* $250

California Locksmiths Association sign. Measures 9" x 16". From the 1940s. *Courtesy of Frank Feher.* $275

Although this Old Coon Cigar sign has seen better days, its eye-catching graphics warrant its inclusion here. It is ink-stamped at bottom right "Balto Enamel & Novelty Company, Baltimore, Maryland." It dates from around 1910. *Courtesy of John Bobroff.* $200.

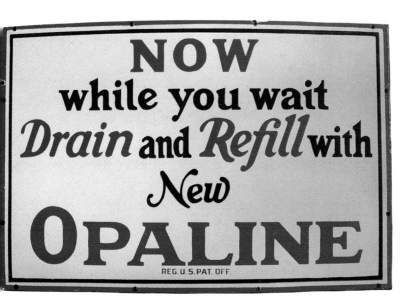

This Opaline sign has to be the world's first "quick change" oil sign. Measures 36" x 24". Dates in the 1930s. *Courtesy of John Bobroff.* $400

Coca-Cola Lunch-Soda sign. Like its twin, these were for drug stores. Measures 18" x 30", and dates in the 1950s. *Courtesy of Dan Reynolds.* $500

Coca-Cola Candy-Films sign. These were meant for small-time drug stores. Measures 18 x 30", and are from the 1950s. They were usually quite thin. *Courtesy of Dan Reynolds.* $500

The DeLaval Cream Separator sign is fairly common. Most of these are somewhat chipped up. The one pictured here is definitely the exception! Measures 16" x 12", and dates in the 1920s. *Courtesy of John Bobroff.* $175

Jervis B. Webb Company sign. A logical choice for a logo! Measures 4"
x 9 1/2", and dates in the 1950s. *Courtesy of Rod Krupka.* $75

Adams Express Money Orders Sold Here strip sign. These are quite scarce. The "sawtooth"
logo was Adams Express Company's trademark. Measures 30" x 3". Dates around 1910.
Author's collection. $900

Schneider's Beverages sign. The gold "medallions" in the center were done by
the lithograph process. Measures 22" x 8", and dates from the 1940s. *Author's
collection.* $300

Headlight Overalls sign. Measures 32" x 10". Dates around the 1920s. *Courtesy
of John Bobroff.* $550

Kirk's Flake Soap sign. Measures 40" x 15". Dates in the 1915 era. *Courtesy of Dan Reynolds.* $800

Ellisons Flower sign. Measures 35 1/2" x 20". Dates around the 1940s. *Courtesy of John Bobroff.* $250

Pacific Electric was a private carrier in the 1920s. Their small logos on each side at the bottom show a bolt of lightning with the words "comfort, speed, safety" encircled around it. *Courtesy of John Bobroff.* $1000.

Pevely Milk used this fantastic multi-colored sign around the 1930s. It measures 17" x 26". Marked at the bottom "AMERICAN VALVE AND ENAMELING CORP." *Private collection.* $2800

Lehigh Valley Egg Producers sign. Measures 13" x 10", and dates to the 1950s. *Courtesy of John Bobroff.* $150

The C.F. & I. sign pictured here has been quite popular because of the logo with three devils. Many coal, furnace and stove manufacturers incorporated devils into their logo. However, most all of their signs were made of tin. Measures 22" x 16". Dates in the 1930s. *Courtesy of John Bobroff.* $500

This notice sign was used as a deterrent to spreading tuberculosis and other diseases. It measures approximately 16" x 12" and dates from the 1920s. *Courtesy of Pete Keim.* $500.

Polarine used this large outside display sign in the 1920s. It measures approximately 5' x 2'. *Courtesy of Ken Fritz at Parkside Antique Mall.* $500

The majority of these Union Pacific signs were in a large size. They were used on bridges. This small version is a great size for the display room, and commands the 1920s. Stamped at the bottom "VERIBRITE CHICAGO". *Courtesy of Bob Knudsen Jr.* $2000

Jewel Coal "octagon" sign. Measures 12" across. Dates from around the 1940s. *Courtesy of John Bobroff.* $150

The Blue Ribbon Malt Extract sign dates from the prohibition era, when "alternatives" to beer were produced. Measures 15" x 22". *Author's collection.* $650

Here's a porcelain sign that can still get its message across even today. It measures approximately 12" x 3" and dates from the 1920s. *Courtesy of Pete Keim.* $200.

Republic Motor Truck sign. Measures 48" x 27". Dates to the 1930s. Marked at the bottom "THIS SIGN IS THE PROPERTY OF REPUBLIC SALES CORPORATION ALABAMA." *Courtesy of John Bobroff.* $400

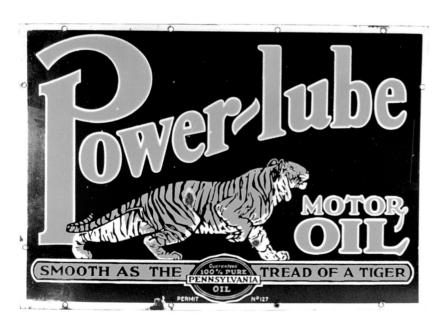

The Power-lube Motor Oil sign. Measures 28" x 20". Dates in the 1920s. Stamped at the bottom. "WOLVERINE PORCELAIN DETROIT THIS IS THE PROPERTY OF THE POWERINE CO." *Courtesy of Mick Hoover.* $750

San Bernardino Valley Transit Co. sign. Measures 18" in diameter, and is from the 1930s. *Courtesy of John Bobroff.* $250

GOLD MEDAL FLOUR

Gold Medal Flour strip sign. Measures 24" x 4", and dates from the 1920s. *Courtesy of Dan Reynolds.* $175

DRINK Pepsi-Cola ICED

Pepsi-Cola incorporated a bottle cap in many of their signs. This 29" x 12" sign dates from the 1950s. Marked "PM/51" at the bottom left. *Courtesy of Dan Reynolds.* $500

This Robert B. Doe Oil Field Service sign features an oil well. Measures 14" in diameter, and dates in the 1950s. *Courtesy of John Bobroff.I* $250

This Pacific Telephone & Telegraph sign is very unusual. Not only is it flat, (vs. being a "hubcap" style as normal) but it measures only 4" in diameter! One of a kind. Dates in the 1920s. *Courtesy of Frank Feher.* $650

This Brandreth's Pills sign not doubt dates prior to 1920. It measures approximately 12" x 3". *Courtesy of Pete Keim.* $300.

Headlight Overalls. Measures 48" x 15". Dates in the 1920s. *Courtesy of John Bobroff.* $550

Early Andersen Window and Door Frame sign. Measures 24" x 24", and is from the 1920s. Marked at the bottom right "VERIBRITE SIGNS CHICAGO BILLY NEWTON CO. MINN. AGENTS." *Author's collection.* $700

United Local-Long Distance sign. Measures 10" in diameter, and dates in the 1930s. Marked "BURDICK—CHI" at the bottom. *Courtesy of Dennis Weber.* $450

Old American Asphalt Singles sign. Measures 24" x 18". Dates from the 1940s. *Courtesy of John Bobroff.* $200

The Ring Bell sign might be the smallest production sign in the world! It's a scant 2" x 2", and dates from around 1920. It has a slightly convex shape. *Courtesy of Dennis Weber.* $40

Hood Tire Dealer die-cut sign. Any time you combine great looking graphics, rarity, and a lot of collectors, then you're going to have a winner. This Hood Tire sign fits the bill! Slightly curved it measures 11 1/2" x 35 1/2", and dates in the 1920s. *Courtesy of Jim Oswald.* $2400

Mansfield's Ice Cream used this sign starting in the 1920s. It measures 30" x 14", and is ink-stamped at the bottom right "BURDICK, CONS. BLDG. CHI". *Private Collection.* $250.

Missouri-Kansas-Texas-Lines sign. Measures 42" x 36". Dates in the 1930s. Marked on the bottom right "VERIBRITE SIGNS CHICAGO." *Courtesy of John Bobroff.* $600

Private Closet 5¢ sign. Measures 12" x 3 1/2". Dates from the 1930s. *Courtesy of Dan Reynolds.* $150

This Bass Shoe sign features the black background in the shape of a shoe. Bass Shoes is one of the few surviving companies that have porcelain advertising dating back eighty years. Measures 18" x 9", and dates around 1910. *Author's collection.* $700

Feen-A-Mint sign. Measures 29" x 7". From the 1940s. Stamped at bottom right "MADE IN USA." *Courtesy of Dan Reynolds.* $200

This Lehigh Anthracite sign is unusual, having the words "and Navigation Co." on it. Thick old porcelain! Measures 21" x 11", and dates in the 1920s. *Courtesy of John Bobroff.* $400

Large Telephone Business Office sign. This one has a stainless steel frame. Measures 36" x 24", and dates from around the 1930s. *Courtesy of Doug MacGillvary.* $600

This Dr. Pepper sign was for use on a cooler. Several slightly different logos were used throughout the years, with this one dating from the 1940s. Measures 26" x 10 1/2". Marked at the bottom right "TEXTILE DALLAS." *Courtesy of Dan Reynolds.* $350

Peter Schuyler Cigar sign. Measures 30" x 12". Dates in the 1930s. Marked at the bottom right "BALTIMORE ENAMEL 200 5TH AVE NY." *Courtesy of John Bobroff.* $200

Alfred Peats Wall Paper used a four-leaf clover as their trademark. Measures 17" x 14". Dates around the 1890s! Stamped at the bottom "B.S. CO. 52 STATE ST. CHI. & HARVEY ILL." *Author's collection.* $300

Lincoln Telephone & Telegraph sign. This has to be one of the most beautiful telephone signs ever made! It certainly is one of the most rare, this 10" x 10" example being one of a kind. It dates from the 1920s, and has also been found in a 16" x 16" size, flanged, two-sided. *Courtesy of Dennis Weber.* $2000

Unusual Ehrlich-Freezer Refrigerator Display Case sign. Measures 25 1/2" x 14", and dates in the 1930s. *Courtesy of Dennis Weber.* $300

Most all the fruit growers in the Pacific Northwest had paper labels that attached to crates ready for shipment. However, few of these operations ever had porcelain signs made. This familiar trademark is the exception. Measures 23" in diameter, and dates in the 1940s. *Courtesy of Rody Cummings.* $750

This Dexter's Mother's Bread sign seems to be designed to represent a chalkboard. It measures approximately 20" x 28" and dates from the 1930s. *Courtesy of John Bobroff.* $400.

Here's one more in a long list of Bond Bread advertising signs. This one dates from the 1930s and measures approximately 20" x 15". *Courtesy of Randy Reith.* $250.

Hyvis Motor Oil sign. Measures 40" x 15", and dates from the 1930s. Marked at bottom right "CAMEO." *Courtesy of John Bobroff.* $350

Lux sign. Measures 24" x 12". Dates in the 1930s. Marked at the bottom left "THE W.F. VILAS CO. LIMITED COWANSVILLE, F.C." The "F.C." stood for French Canada. *Courtesy of Dan Reynolds.* $1100

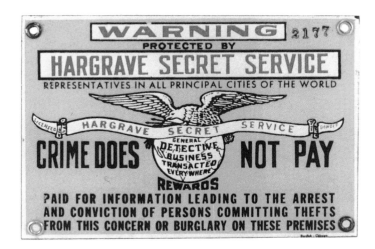

This Hargrave Secret Service sign wanted to make sure an observer would know "crime does not pay." Measures 8" x 5 1/2". Dates from the 1940s. Marked at the bottom right "BURDICK—CHICAGO." *Courtesy of Bernie Nagel.* $75

New-Process Laundry sign. Measures 18" x 10". Dates around the 1920s. *Courtesy of John Bobroff.* $175

Interlines Motor Express sign. Measures 24" x 12". Dates in the 1940s. These were put on the sides of trucks. *Courtesy of Frank Feher.* $200

Carnation Fresh Milk die-cut sign. The advertising from Carnation is very popular with country store item collectors. Measures 14" x 15". Dates in the 1960s. *Courtesy of Rody Cummings.* $500

Die-cut Coca-Cola Fountain Service sign. Measures 23" x 25 1/2". Ink-stamped at the bottom "MADE IN USA 1934 TENN ENAMEL MFG CO. NASHVILLE." *Courtesy of Dan Reynolds.* $1300

This Coca-Cola sign from the 1950s uses a design that collectors call a fishtail—the ends of the sign are rounded inwards. Measures 44" x 16", and dates in the 1950s. *Courtesy of Jim Oswald.* $350

Honest Scrap sign measures 9" x 12", and dates around the turn of the century. *Courtesy of Dan Reynolds.* $600

Railway express went into the Air Express business in 1927. The sign pictured here measures 8" square. *Courtesy of John Bobroff.* $350

Unusual "bull dog" eight-sided sign. These were used by Mack Truck. Measures 6 1/2" across. These date to the 1930s. *Courtesy of Bob Knudsen Jr.* $350

Adams Express Company's Money Orders Sold Here sign. This is the most frequently encountered example of porcelain advertising for Adams Express, but even these are relatively rare. Measures approximately 13" x 10" and is marked at the bottom "F E MARSLAND 84 W. B'WAY. N.Y." *Courtesy of Bill Fraser.* $900

Ford Real Estate die-cut sign. Measures 24" x 21 1/2". Dates from the 1930s. *Courtesy of Rody Cummings.* $350

Pennsylvania Railroad die-cut sign. Dates in the 1940s. Measures 17" x 17". *Courtesy of John Bobroff.* $450

Triton Motor Oil sign. This one appears to have been mounted on a post. Measures 14" in diameter, and dates in the 1950s. *Courtesy of Wendell White.* $400

This 20" diameter Buick Valve In Head sign dates from the 1940s. *Courtesy of John Bobroff.* $400

Damascus used this eye-catching die-cut sign in the 1920s. This company was bought out by Carnation. Measures 17 1/2" x 18". *Private Collection.* $1300.

Here's another example of the many great-looking signs used by Coca-Cola over the years. Measures 27" x 14". Ink-stamped at the bottom "TENN ENAMEL MFG CO. NASHVILLE MADE IN USA 1936." *Courtesy of Dan Reynolds.* $1000

This diamond-shaped sign from REA uses the company's final logo. It measures 11" x 11", and dates from the 1950s. *Author's collection.* $125

This Duke's Mixture sign dates to the 1920s. It measures 5" x 8". *Private Collection.* $550.

You would have to steal a lot of chickens to justify the reward offered by the Poultry Producers of Central California! This unusual sign has a border of small eggs around the edges. It measures 20" x 14", and dates from the 1940s. *Author's collection.* $400

Champion Coal is seen on this two-color rectangle sign from the 1930s. It measures approximately 22" x 13". *Courtesy of John Bobroff.* $100.

Nothing fancy here! Just the facts. Measures 17" x 10", and is from the 1930s. *Courtesy of Frank Feher.* $200

Although the exact location of this thermometer-type reward sign is not known, its message is quite clear. it measures approximately 5" x 20" and dates from the 1920s. *Courtesy of John Romagnoli.* $150.

Lunn Production Service used these three-color signs in the 1950s. No doubt they were mounted to the sides of machinery or trucks. It measures approximately 15" square. *Courtesy of John Bobroff.* $100.

![MAJOR'S CEMENT IS GOOD]

Major's Cement is advertised on this small oval-ended strip sign. It measures a scant 12" x 1" and dates from the 1920s. *Courtesy of Pete Keim.* $75.

Standard Oil of California patented the polar bear trademark. This 3" diameter sign was given to Standard Oil workers and was intended to be fastened to the front of their car. It dates to the 1920s. S.O.E. means "Standard Oil Employee." *Private Collection.* $175.

The unusual nature of this Standard Oil Company sign makes its origin uncertain. However, it could have possibly been used in an overseas location or at an international port area in the United States. It dates from the 1920s and measures approximately 14" x 18". *Courtesy of John Bobroff.* $650.

Canadian National Express was a major railway operation. This two-color square sign was possibly used in terminals or on wagons. It measures approximately 13" x 13" and dates from the 1930s. *Courtesy of John Bobroff.* $400.

This oval Brink's Express Company sign may have found its use on company trucks. One thing for certain, though, the money wasn't far away. It measures approximately 10" x 7" and dates from the 1930s. *Courtesy of Bill and Belinda Fraser.* $350.

Dubbleware Overalls sign. Measures 25" x 8", and dates in the 1940s. Stamped at the bottom right "BURDICK ENAMEL SIGN CO. OF N.E." *Courtesy of Jack Tanner.* $200

This rare Southwestern Bell safety sign was to be used on the back of a truck. The blue letters were silk screened. The remainder was done using a stencil. Measures 5 1/2" in diameter. *Courtesy of Bob Alexander.* $450

H.P Hood & Sons used these beautiful signs on the sides of their milk trucks. It measures 30" in diameter and dates in the 1930s. These signs used three processes in their manufacture; stenciling, silk screening and lithography. *Author's collection.* $3000

This two-color Crystal Laundry Company office sign dates from the 1920s. It measures approximately 18" x 10". *Courtesy of John Bobroff.* $150.

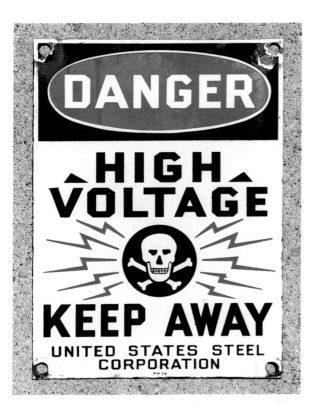

Many industrial companies had their own utility signs. This particular one was used by United States Steel Corporation. It measures approximately 8" x 12". *Courtesy of Rod Krupka.* $75.

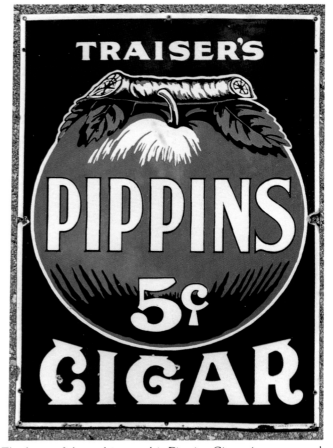

The beautiful graphics on this Pippins Cigar sign are a real eye-catcher. It measures 24" x 34", and is from the 1910 era. Ink-stamped at the bottom "BALTO. ENAMEL & NOV. CO., BALTO. & 107 EUSTIS ST., BOSTON." *Private collection.* $1300

DL&W used this Standard Anthracite sign in the 1940s. It measures approximately 28" x 13". *Courtesy of John Bobroff.* $200.

The beautiful graphics found on this American Eagle Fire Insurance Company sign are a standout. It measures approximately 16" square and dates to around 1925. *Courtesy of John Bobroff.* $750.

Saint Paul Insurance Company sign. Measures 20" x 14", and dates in the 1930s. *Courtesy of Frank Feher.* $275

Sun-Rae Motor Oil oval sign. Measures 42" x 30 1/2", and
dates around the 1930s. *Private collection.* $2000

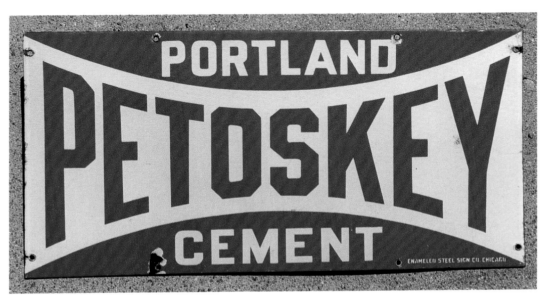

This two-color Petoskey Portland Cement sign measures approximately 25" x
12" and dates to around 1930. *Courtesy of John Bobroff.* $100.

This Duke's Mixture sign has been manufactured so it is raised out at the left side, producing a three-dimensional effect to the package of tobacco. Measures 9" x 12", and dates to around 1910. Marked at the bottom right "BALTO. ENAMEL & NOV. CO., BALTO. & 190 W. B'WAY, N.Y." *Private Collection.* $550

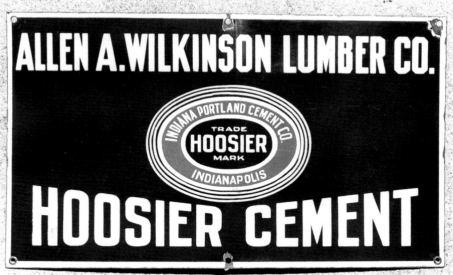

It's amazing the amount of independent advertisers that are found on porcelain signs. The variety is almost endless. This one being from Allen A. Wilkinson Lumber Co. who had their name placed on a Hoosier Cement sign dating from the 1930s. It measures approximately 20" x 12". *Courtesy of John Bobroff.* $150.

This Socony Air-craft Oils sign measures 30" x 20" and dates around 1930. *Courtesy of Larry Burch.* $1600

W. S. Nott Company's Leather Belting. This product was used on machinery that was belt driven from an overhead pulley system. Measures 36" x 12" and dates in the turn of the century. Marked at the bottom right "ENAMELED STEEL SIGN CO. 222 N. STATE ST. CHICAGO." *Author's collection.* $300

Universal Cement strip sign. Measures 19" x 6", and dates in the 1920s. *Courtesy of Ted Tear.* $250

The Vernors sign pictured here is from the side of a cooler. It has a center that is convex in the shape of an oval. Measures 12" x 20", and is from the 1940s. *Courtesy of Ted Tear.* $350

Balsam-Wool Blanket. Measures 36" x 22", and dates around the 1940s. Ink-stamped at the bottom: "VERIBRITE SIGNS, CHICAGO BILLY NEWTON CO., MINN. AGENT." *Courtesy of Larry and Nancy Werner.* $500

This outstanding die-cut Butter Krust Bread sign may have been part of a store display. Another possibility is that it was used on a company truck. Regardless, it's got what it takes! Measures 13" x 18", and dates around 1925. *Courtesy of Gary Metz.* $2800

Chapter Two
FLAT, TWO-SIDED SIGNS

This chapter contains those signs that were manufactured with advertising on both sides. Most of these were to be placed in a stand or frame of some type. This supporting method could be as small as a "lollipop" stand for sidewalk use, or as large as a filling station's main highway sign. Another method used frequently employed an iron bracket. Most of these brackets were simple in construction. However, some are so ornate that you wonder if they took first prize in a blacksmiths' contest!

This Ohio Farmers Insurance Co. sign may be one of a kind. It measures 18" x 14", and dated to around the 1910 era. *Courtesy of Scott Given.* $700

The "deco" style letters could tell even a novice that Kodak had these signs made in the 1930s. This particular sign was done using a stencil, and has a dark blue background. In later years these signs were made with a silk screen and had a noticeably lighter blue background. Measures 20" x 14". *Author's collection.* $1000

This Burdsal's Paints of Durability dates to the 1930s. Measures approximately 15" x 28". *Courtesy of Fred Lupton.* $450.

Castrol Motor oil sign. Measures 22" in diameter. This one dates from the 1940s. *Courtesy of Bob Knudsen Jr.* $200

Nu-Da Paints is features on this 30" x 17" sign dating to the 1930s. *Courtesy of Fred Lupton.* $400

Coreco Motor Oils sign. Measures 30" x 20", and dates from the 1920s. Marked at the bottom right "ING-RICH BEAVER FALLS PA." *Courtesy of Bob Knudsen Jr.* $600

This Conoco Germ Processed Motor Oil sign was designed to go in a triangle-shaped lollipop stand. It dates from the 1930s and measures approximately 24" on each side. *Courtesy of John Bobroff.* $400

California Dairy of Merit sign. Measures 25" x 22", and from the 1940s era. *Courtesy of Ted Tear.* $450

These No Smoking signs were used by Union 76 in the 1950s. They are not common. Measures 15" x 12". *Courtesy of Wendell White.* $350

This Pay Station sign was meant to hang below a telephone sign. Although no company affiliation is obvious, they are attributed to AT&T. Measures 5 1/2" x 18". Dates around 1910. *Author's collection.* $700

Greyhound Atlantic Lines Ticket Office die-cut sign. A beautiful example of the porcelain sign manufacturer's art! More than any other feature, the 1920s bus gives away the age on this one. Measures 25" x 30". *Courtesy of Bob Knudsen Jr.* $2000

Here's another example of super graphics found on paint products signs. This six-color die-cut Martin-Senour hanging sign dates in the 1920s and measures 18" x 22". *Author's collection.* $850

United Motors die-cut sign. This is a scarce variation using a large arrow. Measures 42" x 15". Dates in the 1930s. *Courtesy of Bob Knudsen Jr.* $2600

Western Union oval with arrow. Measures 34" x 21", and dates from the turn of the century. *Author's collection.* $800

Oakland Pontiac Service. Measures 36" x 24". Dates in the 1930s. *Courtesy of Bob Knudsen.* $600

This Paragon Motor Oil sign was designed to be used in a 'lollipop' type stand. They are quite desirable, with the old oil truck, oil well, and refinery being very prominent. Measures 26" in diameter. Dates around the 1920s era. *Courtesy of Jim Oswald.* $2200

Paragon Gasolene used these 26" round lollipop-type signs in the 1920s. Notice the early spelling of gasoline. Marked "NESCO INC. SIGNS N.Y., TOLEDO." *Courtesy of Dave Lane.*

National Automobile Club sign. Measures 29" x 27". Dates in the 1930s. *Courtesy of Bob Knudsen Jr.* $750

Ace High Motor oil oval sign. Measures 23" x 17". Dates around the 1920s era. *Courtesy of Jim Oswald.* $3500

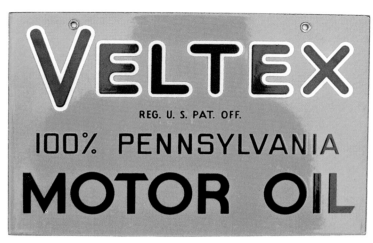

Veltex Motor oil. Measures 11" x 7". Dates around the 1940s. *Courtesy of Wendell White.* $250

Monarch Ranges Authorized Dealer sign. Measures 20" x 17", and dates from the 1920s. *Courtesy of John Bobroff.* $450

This Oak Motor Oil sign was meant to be used in a 'lollipop' stand. Measures 21" in diameter, and dates in the 1920s. *Courtesy of Bob Knudsen Jr.* $1100

Southern Bell Telephone Office oval sign. Measures 34" x 21". Dates between 1921 and 1939. *Private collection.* $700

This die-cut Chevrolet Parts sign was designed to be hung from a bracket. Notice at the bottom that Chevrolet Motor Company wanted people to be sure whose property this was. *Courtesy of Bill Brown.* $700.

Although this Approved Hotel sign dates from the 1940s, the logo found at its center probably has its roots from years much earlier. Notice the spoked wheel used in its center image suggesting a vintage automobile of the early 1900s. *Courtesy of John Bobroff.* $350.

Radiola Dealer die-cut sign. Measures 15" x 19", and is from the 1930s era. Stamped at the bottom "THIS AUTHORIZED SIGN PROPERTY OF THE RADIO CORPORATION OF AMERICA." *Courtesy of John Bobroff.* $800

Pennant Oil sign. Measures 22" x 18". Dates from the 1930s. *Courtesy of John Bobroff.* $450

Famous Reading Anthracite die-cut sign. One more example of the many designs found from those dealing in coal. Measures 24" x 35". Dates from the 1930s. *Courtesy of John Bobroff.* $500

This rare Coca-Cola "Lunch" hanging sign dates in the 1950s. It measures 28" x 28". *Courtesy of Gary Metz.* $1600

This triangular-shaped Seaside Gasoline station sign is from the 1930s. It measures 38" x 38". *Courtesy of John Bobroff.* $800

McCormick-Deering Service oval sign. Measures 32" x 24", and dates from the 1920s. *Author's collection.* $900

AUTHORIZED SERVICE
WHIPPET
AND
WILLYS·KNIGHT
GENUINE PARTS

Whippet and Willys-Knight Authorized Service sign. Measures 36" x 24", and dates in the 1930s. Marked at the bottom "RELIANCE ADVERTISING CO MILWAUKEE." *Courtesy of John Bobroff.* $600

Derby Gasoline station sign. Measures 30" in diameter. This one dates in the 1930s. *Courtesy of John Bobroff.* $450

Intermountain Lines Bus Depot die-cut station sign. The eagle with the mountain background is an eye-catcher! Measures 24" x 19". From the 1920s. *Courtesy of Bob Knudsen Jr.* $2800

This Koolmotor sign was used in a "lollipop" type frame. It dates from the 1930s, and measures 24" in diameter. *Author's collection.* $850

This Wolf's Head Oil sign is a beauty! It measures 30" x 20", and dates around the 1920s era. *Courtesy of Jim Oswald.* $3000

Sterling Motor Oil sign. Measures 30" x 15". From the 1920s. *Courtesy of John Bobroff.* $300

Hudson Parts-Service die-cut sign. Measures 42" x 30". Dates in the 1940s. Marked "AMERICAN" at the bottom right. *Courtesy of John Bobroff.* $850

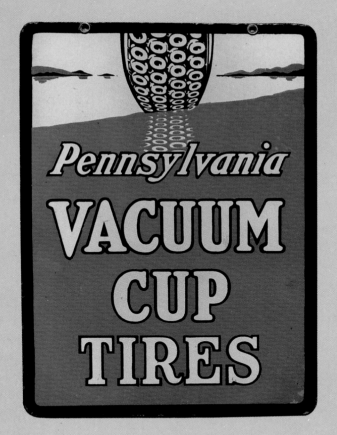

Vacuum Cup Tires were popular in the 1920s. This Pennsylvania Vacuum Cup Tires sign shows a close-up of the patented tread. Measures 16" x 24", and is marked "ING-RICH BEAVER FALLS, PA." *Private Collection.* $900

These Phillips 66 signs were a common sight along America's highways for years. Although they no longer adorn service stations, they have found new homes in collections. Measures 29 1/2" x 29 1/2", and dates in the 1940s. *Courtesy of John Bobroff.* $500

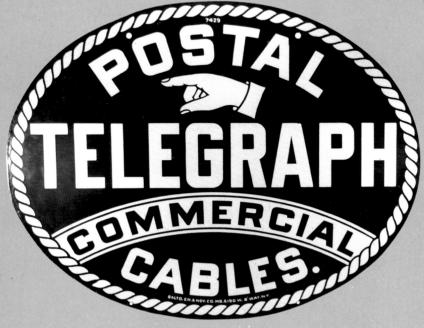

Postal Telegraph Commercial Cables oval sign. The rope border was used on the early Postal Telegraph advertising. The pointing hand is an added plus. Dates around the 1905 era. Measures 30" x 24". Marked at the bottom "BALTO. EN. & NOV. CO. MD. & 190 W. B'WAY, N.Y." *Author's collection.* $1500

General Motors Trucks sign. Measures 30" in diameter. Dates in the 1930s. *Courtesy of John Bobroff.* $450

Sunoco Oil diamond sign. Measures 32 1/2" x 21". Dates around the 1930s. Marked at the bottom "A-715 MADE IN USA." *Courtesy of John Bobroff.* $400

This United Motors oval sign is a scarce one! The two hanging signs fastened below are actually part of the die-cut design, and are not separate signs. Measures 18" x 17", and dates around 1930. *Courtesy of Bob Knudsen Jr.* $2000

Overland Service & Genuine part oval sign. Measures 40" x 30". Dates around the 1930s. Marked at the bottom "L.D. NELKE SIGNS NEW YORK." *Courtesy of Larry and Nancy Werner.* $700

Williams Oil-O-Matic Heating die-cut sign. Measures 24" x 13". Dates around the 1940s. *Courtesy of Bob Knudsen Jr.* $250

Iso-Vis Motor oil sign. Measures 30" in diameter, and dates around the 1930s. Marked at the bottom "RELIANCE ADV CO MILWAUKEE." *Courtesy of John Bobroff.* $450

Most of the signs produced for Jewel Stoves were either flanged or corner signs. This hanging sign dates around 1910, and measures 24" x 24". *Courtesy of John Bobroff.* $550

Motorite die-cut "shield" sign. Measures 19" x 20", and dates in the 1930s. *Courtesy of John Bobroff.* $600

Caterpillar Sales-Service die-cut sign. Measures 27" x 16". Dates around 1930. *Courtesy of Frank Feher.* $450

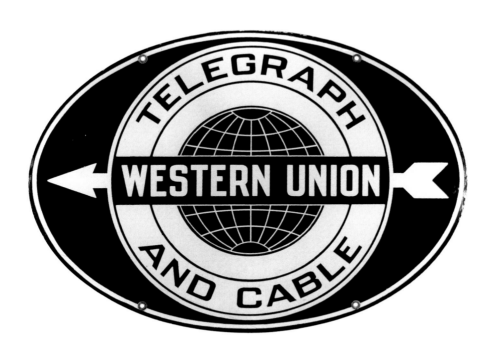

Western Union Telegraph and Cable oval sign. This sign uses the "globe" logo, which was in use around the turn of the century. Measures 31" x 22". *Author's collection.* $2100

Greyhound Lines oval sign. The top of the sign projects up about two inches to accommodate the supports. Measures 36" x 20". This is a later-style logo, and would date around the 1940s. *Courtesy of Frank Feher.* $850

Unusual Standard Ethyl Gasoline sign with the old-style Ethyl logo. Measures 21" x 28", and dates around the 1930s. *Courtesy of John Bobroff.* $350

Shell Oil went through several slight modifications of their logo over the years. This early version dates from the 1920s, and measures 25" x 25". *Courtesy of Frank Feher.* $800

Standard Polarine Gasoline sign. Measures 30" in diameter, and dates in the 1920s. *Courtesy of John Bobroff.* $400

Many cities had their own porcelain signs made up. These were normally placed at the city limits or used as designations for bus stops. This one measures 12" in diameter, and dates from the 1950s. *Courtesy of Frank Feher.* $275

This American Motor Hotel Association sign was produced in the 1950s. Measures 20" in diameter. *Courtesy of Frank Feher.* $200

Unusual Westinghouse Apartments die-cut sign. Measures 19 1/2" x 19" and dates in the 1930s. *Author's collection.* $800

Pan-Am Gasoline & Motor Oils sign. Measures 30" in diameter, and dates in the 1930s. *Courtesy of John Bobroff.* $400

This beautiful porcelain advertisement for Victor Records was made with such detail that it actually has the "grooves"! It measures 28" in diameter, and dates around 1930. Stamped at the bottom "PATENT APPLIED FOR." *Courtesy of Mick Hoover.* $900

Canada Paint used this graphic sign in the 1930s. It measures 14" x 19". *Courtesy of Robert Lloyd.* $350

The Minute Man Service sign pictured here was used by Union 76 in the 1940s. It measures 24" in diameter. *Private collection.* $700

This Genuine Ford Parts oval sign is a favorite among those who collect automobilia. It measures 24" x 10 1/2", and dates from the 1930s era. Ink-stamped at the bottom "VERIBRITE SIGNS, CHICAGO." *Courtesy of Dan Reynolds.* $750

It's hard to imagine any way to make this Sapolin Paints sign more eye-catching! Five colors of porcelain. Measures 26" in diameter, and dates in the 1930s. *Author's collection.* $1900

This 24" round Gulf sign is scarce. It dates from the 1930s. *Courtesy of Dan Reynolds.* $700

Hotel Lee $1 die-cut sign. These are small, measuring only 8 1/2" x 10". Dates around the 1920s. *Courtesy of Dan Reynolds.* $450

Western Union Telegraph and Cable Office oval sign. This scarce sign was also manufactured with the word "Telegraph" in serif-style lettering. As always, the pointing hand is an attention getter. Measures 31" x 22", and dates from the late 1800s. Marked at the bottom "ING-RICH, BEAVER FALLS,PA. 100. WILLIAM ST. N.Y." *Author's collection.* $1900

This is a scarce Coca-Cola sign. It measures 26 1/2" x 25", and is marked at the bottom left "MADE IN USA 1939." *Courtesy of Dan Reynolds.* $1200

This unusual Beaver-Penn Motor oil sign dates from the 1930s. The sign has a beaver in the oval at the top, and at the bottom left there is a not-so-handsome canine with the slogan "The watchdog of your motor." Measures 22" x 18". *Courtesy of Bob Knudsen Jr.* $500

Any Indian chief in full head dress commands attention! This 48" round Wasatch sign is a beauty. It dates in the 1930s. *Courtesy of Bob Knudsen Jr.* $2700

Here's a fabulous 1935 era die-cut Coca-Cola sign. Measures 24 1/2" x 22". These are quite scarce, especially in such choice condition. *Courtesy of Dan Reynolds.* $4500

This rare Central Office sign has a metal frame around the edge of the sign. Measures 22" x 29", and dates around 1910. *Author's collection.* $1400

The Hains-CeBrook Ice Cream sign was used in a sidewalk stand. Measures 20" x 28". Dates around the 1920s. *Author's collection.* $600

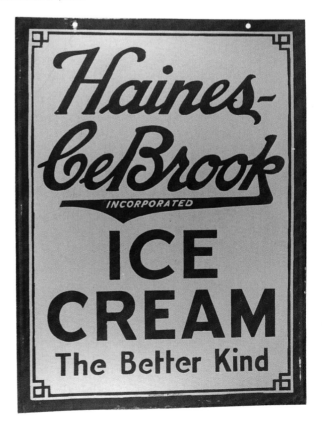

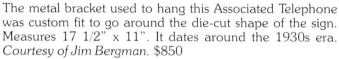

The metal bracket used to hang this Associated Telephone was custom fit to go around the die-cut shape of the sign. Measures 17 1/2" x 11". It dates around the 1930s era. *Courtesy of Jim Bergman.* $850

Beacon Penn Motor Oil sign. Measures 30" x 30". Dates around the 1930s. *Courtesy of John Bobroff.* $400

Kurfees Paints sign. Measures 30" x 20". Dates from around 1940. *Author's collection.* $350

These Lawrence Tiger Brand Paint signs are not rare, but their great-looking graphics keeps them in high demand. They are also found with a red background color instead of yellow. Measures 17" x 23", and dates from the 1940s. *Author's collection.* $700

This Conoco Gasoline sign with the "minute man" logo has to be one of the most sought-after advertising pieces for "petro" collectors. It measures 25" in diameter, and dates in the 1920s. The "minute man" was done using the lithographic process. *Courtesy of Bob Knudsen Jr.* $2400

This Michigan Road Atlas was published as a fishing and hunting guide. The copyrights for the map were secured from Rand McNally, and their logo was prominently placed on the front cover. Any time a porcelain sign is found in paper advertising you have the makings for a great go-with. *Author's collection.*

Omar Gasoline made sure the motorists knew their fuel contained Ethyl. Measures 30" in diameter and dates around 1930. *Courtesy of Archer Classic Cars.* $550

As far as *eye*-appeal goes, this Rand McNally hanging sign has plenty to offer! It's die-cut in the shape of an arrowhead. It shows an American Indian. To top it all off, there are no fewer than six colors of porcelain. Definitely an *eye*-opener! Measures 13 1/2" x 17", and dates in the 1920s. *Author's collection.* $4000

Check Parcels Here hanging sign. This one measures 16" x 5", and is from the 1920s. *Courtesy of the Railroad Memories Museum, Spooner, Wisconsin.* $450

Hudson Authorized Service 42" diameter station sign. Dates from the 1940s. *Courtesy of Larry and Nancy Werner.* $850

This 36" in diameter Blue Seal Motor Oil sign was produced by the Illinois Agricultural Association. Dates around the 1940s. *Courtesy of Larry and Nancy Werner.* $600

Red Crown Gasoline by Standard Oil Company of Nebraska. Measures 22" x 18", and dates in the 1920s. *Private collection.* $1450

Chapter Three
FLANGED TWO-SIDED SIGNS

All signs in this chapter were designed with a built-in side mount that is called a flange. Normally, this amounts to no more than a ninety-degree bend on one edge of the sign. There are some other things that have shown up though, such as the "split flange" system used on some Western Union signs.

Many times the only damage to a sign will be limited to the flange area. Unless it is severe, this should not count heavily in the grading or the value of a sign. The face of a sign has the advertising—not the flange.

Be careful to inspect flat two-sided signs, as it may prove to have been a flanged sign that had the flange carefully cut off. Normally, small chips will follow the edge that the saw blade went along, and no porcelain will be evident along the edge as well.

This is a one-of-a-kind sign from United Telephone & Telegraph Company. Measures 17" x 18", and dates around the turn of the century. Marked at the bottom right "BRILLIANT MFG. CO. PHILA. PA." *Courtesy of Dennis Weber.* $1500

Arden Milk Company used this great looking die-cut sign in the 1930s. It measures 24" x 36". *Private Collection.* $2500

Havoline Motor Oil sign. Measures 13" x 20". Dates in the 1940s. *Courtesy of Bob Knudsen Jr.* $1300

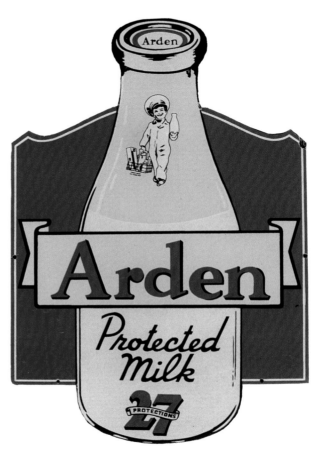

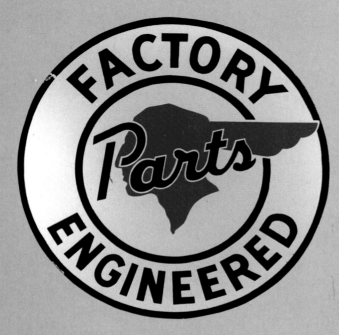

REDUCE PLOWING COST USE HAYNES STELLITED SHARES

This die-cut Haynes Stellited Shares sign dates around 1910. It measures 5 1/2" x 18". *Courtesy of Ted Tear.* $300

The Factory Engineered Parts sign pictured here was from a Pontiac dealership. Measures 20" in diameter. Dates in the 1940s. *Courtesy of Bob Knudsen Jr.* $900

Ingersoll watch die-cut sign. These are from the 1910 era. Measures 16" x 9". *Courtesy of John Bobroff.* $350

This Kendall Penzbest Motor Oils sign dates from the 1930s. It measures approximately 20" in diameter. *Courtesy of Tom Licouris.* $500.

Here's another one of the many variations found in the Headlight Overalls signs. It measures 18" x 12", and dates around 1920. Marked at the bottom "BEATTY McMILLAN COMPANY DETROIT." *Courtesy of John Bobroff.* $500

The New England Telephone & Telegraph Company was a prolific advertiser. This example measures 17" x 20", and dates around 1910. It is marked at the bottom right "BALTO. ENAMEL & NOV. CO. BALTO & 190 W. B'WAY. N.Y." *Private collection.* $650

The Portland Speed Cement is reported to be from Speed, Indiana. Measures 10" in diameter, and dates from the 1930s. *Courtesy of John Bobroff.* $175

Texaco had these die-cut signs manufactured for them in the 1920s. Measures 18" x 23". *Author's Collection.* $1300.

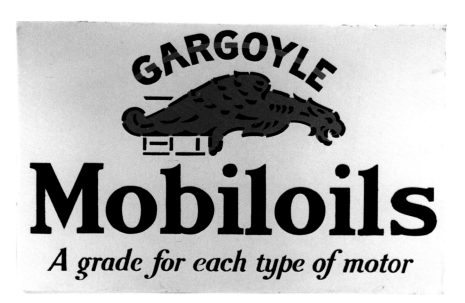

The predecessor to the Mobil "flying horse" trademark was the Gargoyle. Many different signs through the years used this logo. The one pictured here measures 24" x 16", and dates around 1930. *Author's collection.* $550

This Hair Bobbing sign dates in the 1930s. It measures 24" x 12". *Courtesy of Mick Hoover.* $250

This early Buck's Brilliantene Oil sign dates in the 1890s. It measures 28" x 18". *Author's collection.* $2200

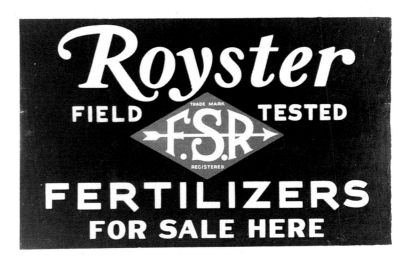

Postal Telegraph Send Your Telegrams Here sign. Measures 14" x 15 1/2", and dates from the 1920s. *Courtesy of Mick Hoover.* $450

Royster Fertilizers sign. Measures 18 1/2" x 12", and dates from around the 1940s. *Private collection.* $200

Coca-Cola Sold Here die-cut sign. Measures 17" x 20", and is from the 1930s. *Courtesy of Dan Reynolds.* $950

This Red Devil Cement sign has a logo you won't forget! Measures 12" x 20", and dates in the 1920s. *Courtesy of Rody Cummings.* $850

Good Year had a winner with this great looking die-cut motorcycle tires sign. It measures 24" x 17", and dates to the 1920s. *Private Collection.* $4500.

The Interstate Utilities Company Public Telephone sign. Measures 12" x 14", and dates in the 1920s. *Author's collection.* $1200

This Columbia Records sign has a "floating" record in the center! It measures 16" x 24", and dates from the 1930s. *Courtesy of Dan Reynolds.* $2700

PITTSBURGH PAINTS

Here's Pittsburgh Paints doing what it does best: color! Eleven colors in all. Done with a silk screen process. Measures 25" x 16". Dates in the 1950s. *Author's collection.* $250

DOMINION EXPRESS MONEY ORDERS ISSUED HERE.

ACTON BURROWS CO TORONTO

Dominion Express Money Orders sign. The unusual flange was designed to lay "flat" with the rest of the sign. This may have been a promotional feature, but it no doubt restricted the ability to mount the sign in many instances. Measures approximately 22" x 14", and dates around 1900. Marked at the bottom right "ACTON BURROWS CO. TORONTO." *Courtesy of Bill Fraser.* $600

The Independent Telephone Association's red, white and blue shield logo was used on this 18" x 18" sign for The Home Telephone Company. It dates to around 1910, and is stamped at the bottom "BURDICK, CONSUMER'S BLDG., CHI." *Private Collection.* $700

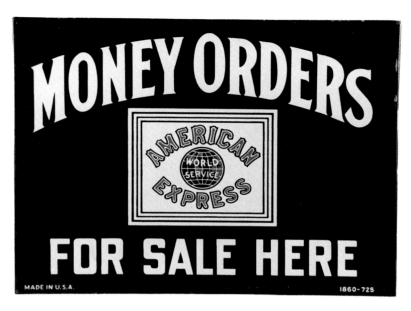

This American Express Money Orders sign dates in the 1920s. It measures 18" x 14". Marked at the bottom "BALTIMORE ENAMEL & NOV. CO. BALTO. & 200 FIFTH AVE N.Y." *Author's collection.* $775

Red Cross Stoves & Ranses sign. Measures 13" x 13", and dates around 1910. Marked at the bottom right "BALTO ENAMEL AND INK COMPANY." *Courtesy of John Bobroff.* $400

Unusual Sherwin-Williams "Opex" paint sign. Measures 22" x 16". Dates from around the 1930s. Marked at the bottom "BALTO ENAMEL & NOV. CO. BALTO & 200 FIFTH AVE. N.Y." *Author's collection.* $550

The Western Union Telephone Your Telegrams Here sign incorporates a "candle stick" style telephone into the graphics. Naturally, this helps date the sign to the 1920s era. This sign uses a "split flange" for its support system. Measures 18" x 19 1/2", and is also found in a smaller, more scarce version. *Author's collection.* $1100

This Masury Paint Store sign dates around 1940. It measures 24" x 16". Ink-stamped "SMANK SIGN CO. N.Y." *Author's collection.* $550

Like many other paint companies, Pierce's Paints found that using a paint can on their sign worked the best. This one measures 18" x 20", and is from the 1920s. *Author's collection.* $450

Interstate Telephone used a telephone pole for its logo. Measures 17 1/2" x 12", and dates from around 1930. *Author's collection.* $675

Many states had their own motorist associations. This die-cut sign from Wisconsin was placed at locations that serviced cars. It's unusual to find the date placed on a sign, as it limited its usefulness, in this case to only the year 1922. Measures 20" in diameter. *Author's collection.* $1200

This Bird Roofs sign dates from the 1930s. Note that the company was established in 1795! Measures 14" x 20". *Author's collection.* $500

Gold Leaf Shoes die-cut sign. Measures 21" x 13". Dates from the 1930s. *Courtesy of Ted Tear.* $350

The Peninsular Paint Company was located in Detroit, Michigan. The sign pictured here has a large paint can with the lower peninsula of Michigan as their logo. Measures 14 1/2" x 20". These date to around 1915. *Author's collection.* $750

This Independent Telephone Pay Station sign is from Pennsylvania. Measures 18" x 18", and dates from around 1910. Ink-stamped at the bottom "ING. RICH. BEAVER FALLS, PA." *Author's collection.* $1250

This scarce Cumberland Telephone and Telegraph sign has white stars and a "modified" bell. Measures 18" x 21", and dates from around 1910. Stamped at the bottom "BALTO ENAMEL & NOV. CO." *Private collection.* $900

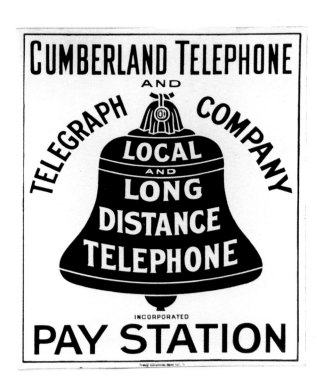

Several of these beautiful Cumberland Telephone & Telegraph Company signs were turned up in a warehouse find a few years ago. All were made form heavy old rolled iron. These date from around 1910, and measures 18" x 22". Ink-stamped at the bottom "ING. RICH. BEAVER FALLS, PA." *Private collection.* $850

Tri-State Telephone and Telegraph Company sign with the independent shield. Measures 18" x 18", and dates from around 1920. Marked at the bottom "B.S. CO. STATE ST. CHI. & BEAVER FALLS, PA." *Courtesy of Dennis Weber.* $800

The use of the polar bear on this die-cut Zerolene sign made it a real *eye-catcher*! Measures 23" x 20". It dates around the 1920s. *Courtesy of John Bobroff.* $2000

Billings-Chapin die-cut paint sign. The sailor boy is a real *eye-catcher*. Measures 21 1/2" x 24", and dates around the 1930s. *Author's collection.* $850

This De Laval Agency sign is a great looking country store advertising piece! Some of the finer print work was done by the silk screen process. Measures 18" x 26 1/2". Dates from the turn of the century. These are also found in a *newer* variation that has a light blue background color. *Author's collection.* $1400

This RPM Motor Oil sign dates in the 1930s. It measures 22" in diameter. *Courtesy of John Bobroff.* $400

The red, white and blue shield was the trademark of the Independent Telephone Association. This colorful sign was used by the hundreds throughout the country. However, relatively few have survived. Measures 18" x 18", and dates in the 1910 era. *Author's collection.* $800

Kearney Steam Laundry sign. Measures 14" x 10". This dates around 1910. Ink-stamped at the bottom "BS COMPANY 52 STATE STREET CHI. BALTO E & N CO. BALTO." *Courtesy of John Bobroff.* $200

Many states had tourist associations to promote travel. The sign pictured here was on a hotel in Michigan's upper peninsula. Measures 14" x 18". Dates from the 1930s. *Author's collection.* $850

Supreme Auto Oil is featured on this early Gulf Refining Company sign. Notice the logo at left which has an early automobile radiator superimposed on a spoked wheel. *Courtesy of Bill and Belinda Fraser.* $450

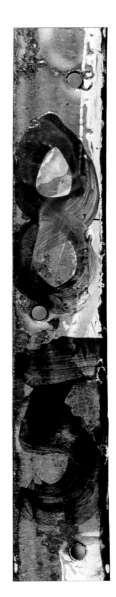

Here's a shot of the flange on the Voigt's Flour sign. You would be hard pressed to find another sign with "85" finger scribed into the potential! The sign was manufactured in England by Imperial Enamel which had opened an office in New York city by 1885. *Courtesy of Dave and Beth Justice.*

This William Penn Motor Oils sign dates from the 1920s. It measures 18" in diameter. *Courtesy of John Bobroff.* $450

Railway Express Agency sign. Measures 12" x 14". These date to the 1930s. *Author's collection.* $650

Telephone Pay Station sign. This has heavy porcelain, but they were also made in a newer look-alike that had thinner porcelain and is much more common. Measures 18" x 8", and dates around 1910. *Author's collection.* $1000

This Michigan Bell Authorized Agency sign was used at locations where you could pay your telephone bill. Measures 12" x 15", and dates from the 1940s. *Author's collection.* $500

Peninsular Furnaces, Stoves and Ranges sign. Measures 16" x 23 1/2". These date from around 1910. Ink-stamped at the bottom "B.S. CO. 52 STATE ST. CHI. & BEAVER FALLS, PA." *Author's collection.* $1100

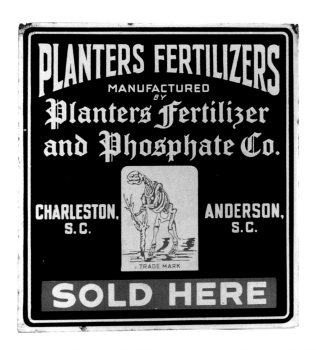

This unusual Planters Fertilizers sign uses a dinosaur skeleton for a trade mark. Measures 16" x 18", and dates around the 1930s. *Courtesy of John Bobroff.* $550

Peoples Coal Company wanted everyone to know that J.L.
Green was their Manager. This dates from the 1920s era, and
measures 20" x 12". Marked at the bottom "ING-RICH
BEAVER FALLS PA." *Courtesy of John Bobroff.* $250

Only a few of these Dakota Central
Telephone Company signs are known to
exist. These are unusual in that they feature
a Local & Long Distance bell and a red
and white shield, which is the trademark
of the Independent Telephone Association.
Measures 18" x 18", and dates around
1910. Marked at the bottom right
"BURDICK CONS. BLDG. CHI." *Author's
collection.* $2100

Monarch Paint Sold Here sign. Measures 19" x 14". These
are from the 1930s era. *Author's collection.* $500

These Peninsular Telephone Company Pay Station signs date
to the 1920s era. They measure 14" x 8". *Private collection.*
$850

Whitman's Chocolates & Confection Agency sign. Measures 10" x 20", and dates in the 1940s. *Courtesy of Ted Tear.* $350

This distinctive Socony die-cut sign is a stand-out in the crowd. Although many of these were produced, few are around in this condition. Measures 20" x 24", and dates from the 1920s. *Author's collection.* $950

Even a novice would have little trouble dating this sign to the 1920s era. The woman's dress and hair style make it obvious. Unlike Monarch Paints, the Sapolin Company likes to divert from the company's logo as the central theme on many of its signs. This one measures 12" x 20", and has marked at the bottom "BALTO ENAMEL & NOV. CO. BALTO & 200 FIFTH AVE. N.Y." *Author's collection.* $900

113

Supreme Auto Oil sign. Measures 22" x 18". Dates from the 1920s. Ink-stamped at the bottom "CRICHTON CURL ENAMEL CO. ELLWOOD CITY PA." *Author's collection.* $650

This Indiana Telephone Pay Station sign is believed to be the only one known. Measures 12" x 12 1/2", and dates from the 1930s era. *Author's collection.* $1200

This Hanna's Green Seal Paints sign dates from the 1920s. The small green seal in the paint can required a separate stencil for that color as well as another run through the firing oven! Measures 19" x 14". *Author's collection.* $600

Telephone Pay Station sign. Measures 16" x 20". Dates from the turn of the century. Ink-stamped at the bottom "INGRAM RICHARDSON BEAVER FALLS, PA. & 100 WILLIAM ST., N.Y." *Author's collection.* $900

Klein had this sign made around 1915. It measures 22" x 8".
Klein Tools is still in business today. *Courtesy of Dennis Weber.*
$500

Lincoln Paints used this attention getter around
the 1915 era. It measures 15" x 20". Marked
at the bottom "B.S. CO. 166 N. STATE ST.
CHI. & BALTO. ENL. & NOV. CO., MD."
Private Collection. $800

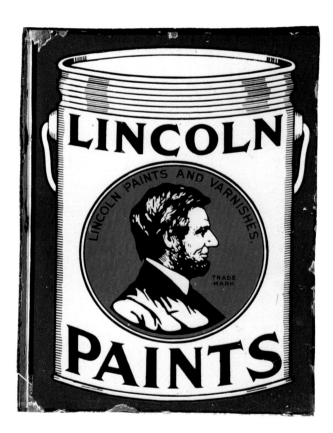

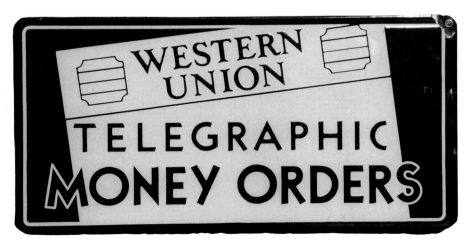

Western Union used this split-flange sign int he
1930s. It measures 18" x 9". *Private Collection.* $350

Lincoln Telephone & Telegraph Company produced this colorful sign with a candlestick telephone in the 1920s. It measures 16" x 16". *Author's collection.* $2000

This unusual Sylvan Kerosene Oil sign dates from around 1930. It measures approximately 20" x 16". *Courtesy of John Bobroff.* $650.

Monogram Greases-Oils. These are normally found with a thick porcelain coating. Measures 24" x 15", and dates in the 1920s. *Author's collection.* $550

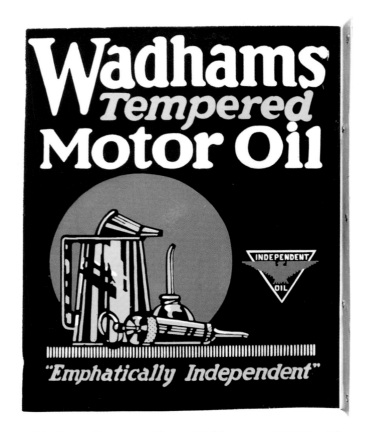

This rare American Railway Express sign was used in the 1920s. It measures approximately 16" x 12", and is marked "BURDICK AMERICAN BLDG., CHI. & BALT. ENML. & NOV. CO. MD." *Courtesy of Bill Fraser.* $950

Wadhams Tempered Motor Oil. Measures 16 1/2" x 20 1/2". Dates in the 1920s. *Author's collection.* $2300

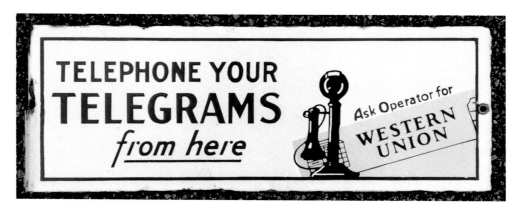

This "slit flange" Western Union sign is rare. It measures 20" x 7", and dates in the 1920s. *Courtesy of Kim & Mary Kokles.* $750

Lowe Brothers used this blue & white flanged sign to advertise their paints in the 1920s. It measures 14" x 22", and is ink-stamped "INGRAM-RICHARDSON BEAVER FALLS, PA." *Courtesy of Dave Beck.* $450

Here's another example of the fine graphics found on many of the paint manufacturers' signs. This on measures 16" x 24", and is from the 1930s. Ink stamped at the bottom right "L.D. NELKE SIGNS, NEW YORK." *Author's collection.* $800

Chapter Four
CURVED SIGNS

This chapter contains signs that were designed to "go around" something. Normally this would be the corner of a building. This was quite common during the early part of this century. A special mounting bracket was employed to the corner of a building, and the sign fastened to the bracket. Curved signs had other uses as well, such as being found on telephone poles or street light posts. Some companies had their curved signs "tailor fit" to go right on the product being advertised. As an example a root beer sign to be fastened to a dispenser.

This beautiful Acorn Stoves and Ranges sign dates around 1910. It measures 15" x 20 1/2". Ink-stamped at the bottom right "MARYLAND ENAMEL & SIGN CO. BALTO. MD." *Author's collection.* $1800

The Lash's Root Beer sign pictured here was used on a soda fountain root beer dispenser. It measures 16" x 7", and is from the 1930s. *Author's collection.* $600

West Bend Lithia Beer sign. The use of black porcelain really helped make the colors come alive! Measures 17" x 14". This dates in the 1930s. Ink-stamped at the bottom right "BURDICK, CHI." *Author's collection.* $600

The Brazil Brewing Company of Brazil, Indiana used this spectacular sign to advertise its product around 1910. Several of these were turned up in a warehouse find. Measures 12" x 20". Ink-stamped at the bottom right "B.S.CO. 52 STATE ST. CHI. & BALTO. E & N CO MD." *Author's collection.* $1600

The Miller sign was probably more plentiful than any other of the curved beer signs. However, not all of them would still look this nice! Measures 17" x 14", and is from the 1930s. Ink-stamped at the bottom right "BURDICK ENAMEL SIGN CO.—CHICAGO & BALTO." *Author's collection.* $450

This is one of the few porcelain signs that can still be found in service today. It seems like almost every barber shop had a sign similar to one of these. The William Marvey Company was the distributor, not the manufacturer. They sold supplies to the trade and can still be found today in St. Paul, Minnesota. Measures 15" x 24", and dates in the 1950s. *Courtesy of Dan Reynolds.* $250

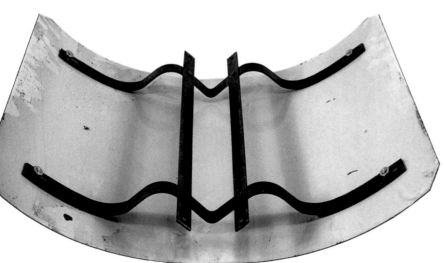

This is the original mounting bracket still on the back of the Miller sign. Nearly all curved signs utilized a support system similar to this.

Peninsular Furnaces, Stoves and Ranges sign. This measures 17" x 24", and dates form the turn of the century. Marked at the bottom right "FMB CO 52 STATE ST. CHICAGO." *Courtesy of John Bobroff.* $500

Any cigar that cost 10¢ when this sign was manufactured was an expensive smoke! Likewise, any six-color curved porcelain sign was sure to be high-priced as well. Jas. McGahan & Bro. seem to have gotten their money's worth though, as this super Prof. Morse Perfecto advertisement demonstrates. Measures 11" x 16", and dates around 1915. Ink-stamped at the bottom "BALTO ENL. & NOV. CO. MD 190 W. B'WAY., N.Y." *Author's collection.* $1900

The Shine corner sign pictured here measures 6" x 52"! It dates in the 1920s. *Courtesy of John Bobroff.* $800

False alarms were a problem even years ago. This little reward sign was fastened to fire alarm call boxes. Measures 7" x 10", and dates in the 1930s. *Courtesy of John Bobroff.* $150

These two Blatz signs are an example of the similarities that can be found among the thousands of porcelain signs manufactured over the years. They both measure 15" x 17 1/2", and date to around the 1930s. *Courtesy of Bob Knudsen Jr.* $800 ea.

 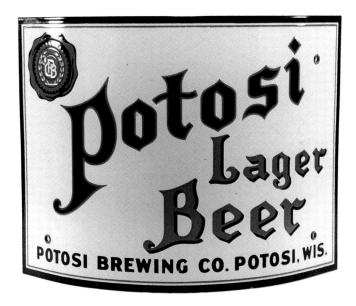

It seems like the list of Wisconsin breweries goes on and on. Pictured here is one from the Potosi Brewing Company, from Potosi, Wisconsin. Measures 17" x 14". Dates around the 1930s. *Author's collection.* $500

This Campbell's Soup sign is an outstanding example of "country store" advertising. Measures 13" x 22 1/2", and dates to the 1920s. *Author's Collection.* $2700

Rahr's Elk's Head Beer of Oshkosh sign. Measures 17" x 14". Dates in the 1930s. Ink-stamped at the bottom right "BURDICK, CHI." *Author's collection.* $500

This O'Sullivan's Heels sign dates from the 1920s. It measures 13 1/2" x 16". *Private collection.* $550

Old Dutch Cleanser used this great looking corner sign starting around 1910. It measures 19" x 32", and is stamped at the bottom "ING-RICH BEAVER FALLS, PA." *Private Collection.* $1600

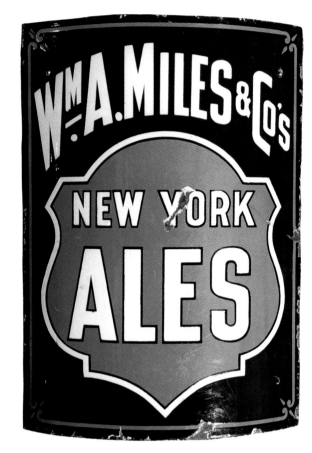

This super little die-cut curved sign was on a Peerless scale. The beautiful graphics used to create the policeman were done using a litho process. Notice that even the shadow was important. A real work of art! Measures 5" x 9", and dates from around the 1920s. *Courtesy of Bob Knudsen Jr.* $500

Few porcelain signs have been found advertising ales. This William A. Miles & Co. example is an early one, dating to around 1890. It measures 18" x 24". *Author's collection.* $550

This Pedestrian Safety Zone oval sign was no doubt mounted to light posts. It measures approximately 16" x 7" and dates from the 1930s. *Courtesy of John Bobroff.* $300

Here's a close-up of a stamping found on the back side of a Sweet-Orr sign. Markings like these are quite scarce, as most businesses figured their signs were going out for a one-way trip!

Hamm's Beer on tap sign. Measures 17" x 14", and dates around the 1940s. Stamped at the bottom "BURDICK ENAMEL SIGN CO., CHICAGO & BALTO." *Courtesy of Tom and Sherry Watt.* $500

Kendall The 2000 Mile Oil sign. Measures 20" x 34", and dates in the 1940s. *Courtesy of Kim and Mary Kokles.* $1250

Peoples Duluth Beer was made with "chemically pure" Lake Superior water. How times have changed! Measures 20" x 14", and dates in the 1930s. *Courtesy of Mervin Eisel.* $600

Chapter Five
GASOLINE PUMP SIGNS

So many different gasolines were manufactured through the years, each with their own trade name, that a separate chapter is appropriate to deal with the many designs and companies that are found on pump signs.

Some of these are of a more common nature, produced in the thousands. Others are rare, with only a few examples known. Generally, the most difficult type of pump signs to obtain are from marine and aviation use. These were found at relatively few locations.

This Bulko Gasoline die-cut sign features an elephant. Measures 12 1/2" x 11". Dates from the 1930s. *Courtesy of Bob Knudsen Jr.* $1400

Time Super Gasoline. Measures 9" x 14". Dates in the 1950s. *Courtesy of Frank Feher.* $350

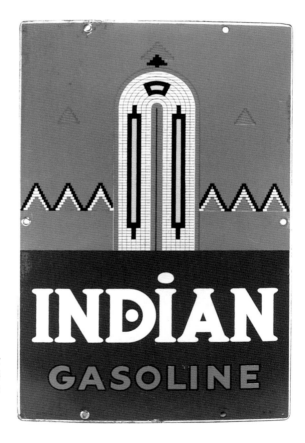

These Indian Gasoline signs are fairly common, but their unusual graphics have kept them in high demand. Measures 12" x 18", and dates in the 1940s. Marked "3-41" on the bottom. *Courtesy of Rod Krupka.* $200

Shell Premium Gasoline die-cut sign. The red background on the Shell trade mark was in use for only a short time. These date to the 1930s, and measure 12" x 12". Marked at the bottom "MADE IN USA." *Courtesy of Bob Knudsen Jr.* $1200

Tydol Flying A sign. Measures 10" in diameter. Dates around the 1940s. *Courtesy of Rod Krupka.* $150

Keystone Powerfuel sign. Measures 12" x 14", and dates from the 1950s. Marked at the bottom right "I R 55". *Courtesy of John Bobroff.* $200

Texaco Sky Chief with Petrox sign. Measures 12" x 22". Dates from the 1950s. Marked at the bottom "MADE IN USA 9-1-55." *Courtesy of Rod Krupka.* $125

Hypower Fina Gasoline die-cut sign. Measures 11" x 13 1/2". Dates in the 1950s. *Courtesy of John Bobroff.* $200

This 'A' with wings is from Flying A Petroleum. Measure 13 1/2" x 9", and dates around the 1940s. *Courtesy of Wendell White.* $800

A rare six-inch Shell sign with black background. This may have been used on truck doors or employee's vehicles. Dates from the 1920s era. Also found in a ten-inch version. *Courtesy of Bob Knudsen Jr.* $1200

This Gloco Super Ethyl die-cut sign dates in the 1950s. It measures 15" x 9 1/2". Marked at the bottom "Mc AX." *Courtesy of Frank Feher.* $150

Sinclair H-C Gasoline sign. Measures 14" x 14". Dates in the 1920s. Marked at the bottom right "SINCLAIR CDHC-1." *Courtesy of Jim Oswald.* $800

The old-style Ethyl logo is used on this Southland sign from the 1930s era. Measures 12" x 12". *Courtesy of Rod Krupka.* $150

The Husky Hi Power sign dates in the 1950s. Measures 14" x 15". *Courtesy of Bob Knudsen Jr.* $900

This rare Golden Eagle sign dates in the 1940s. Measures 13" x 13". *Courtesy of Bob Knudsen Jr.* $900

United Hi-Spirit 10" round sign. This dates around the 1940s. *Courtesy of Bob Knudsen Jr.* $550

This 12" round Signal Ethyl uses the newer style Ethyl logo. Dates in the 1940s. *Courtesy of Bob Knudsen Jr.* $800

This Fuel Oil sign was used by Sinclair Petroleum. It measures 12" x 12", and dates around the 1930s. Marked at the bottom right "VERIBRITE SIGNS—CHICAGO." *Courtesy of Wendell White.* $450

Sterling Super Blend sign. Measures 12" x 15", and is from the 1960s. *Courtesy of Rod Krupka.* $90

This Cargray Gold sign is from the 1940s. What's unusual is that the marking "VERIBRITE SIGNS—CHICAGO" is on the back side. Measures 10" in diameter. *Courtesy of Rod Krupka.* $200

Blue Sunoco 200X die-cut sign. The "X" on the sign is a self-adhesive decal, not porcelain. Measures 15" x 21", and dates in the 1940s. *Courtesy of Mick Hoover.* $200

The Texaco Diesel Chief pictured here dates from the 1960s. They were also manufactured in a more scarce green version, as well as a rare yellow version. Measures 12" x 18". *Courtesy of Rod Krupka.* $150

This Jenney Aero sign is rare. The word "solvenized" seems to be a trade name coined by Jenney Manufacturing. Measures 12" in diameter, and dates around the 1930s era. *Courtesy of Barry Baker.* $3000

This Sinclair sign dates from the 1960s. Reportedly, only twenty-five were produced by Southwest Porcelain in Tulsa, Oklahoma. Measures 7 1/2" x 7". *Courtesy of Wendell White.* $350

Sinclair Pennsylvania Motor Oil 11" round sign. This has the "older" style dinosaur. Dates in the 1920s. Marked at the bottom "SINCLAIR SP-2." *Courtesy of Bob Knudsen.* $800

This die-cut shield sign has the unmistakable pegasus logo of Mobil. However, having only the horse on one of these is rare. Measures 9" x 8 1/2", and dates in the 1950s. *Courtesy of Bob Knudsen Jr.* $800

This Laureleaf curved pump sign was photographed on a shed in central Idaho. The large "75" indicated its octane rating. Measures approximately 12" round. Dates in the 1930s. *$300*

Here's a "pair" of signs from Union 76. The 76 Plus Gasoline was test-marketed in Salt Lake City in 1967 & 1968, and then abandoned. Measures 11 1/2" in diameter. *Courtesy of Wendell White.* $200 ea.

The Red Crown Gasoline sign pictured here was mounted near the top of "visible" style gas pumps. The patent date is October 12, 1915. Measures 14" in diameter. *Courtesy of Bob Knudsen Jr.* $800

Texaco used these familiar signs for years. They were produced in several sizes, the most common being 12" x 18". The one pictured here is scarce, measuring only 8" x 12". These date from the 1950s. Marked at the bottom right "P&M 4-55." *Courtesy of Rod Krupka.* $150

Flying "A" Ethyl Gasoline sign. Measures 10" x 10", and dates in the 1940s. *Courtesy of Mick Hoover.* $300

This rare Green Streak Gasoline sign from Shell Oil dates from the 1930s. Measures 12" in diameter. *Courtesy of Bob Knudsen Jr.* $1450

This Texaco die-cut sign was for the side of delivery trucks. Measures 10 1/2" x 12", and is from the 1950s. Marked at the bottom is "10-5-52." *Courtesy of Bob Knudsen Jr.* $375

Shamrock Kerosene sign. Measures 10 1/2" x 12 1/2", and is from the 1950s. *Courtesy of Rod Krupka.* $150

Golden West Oil Company sign. Measures 10" in diameter. Dates in the 1950s. *Courtesy of Bob Knudsen Jr.* $600

The graphics on this Smith-O-Lene Aviation Brand Gasoline sign are outstanding! It measures 10" in diameter, and dates from the 1940s. Marked on the reverse side "VERIBRITE SIGNS—CHICAGO." *Courtesy of Bob Knudsen Jr.* $1300

Mobilgas Aircraft die-cut shield sign. Measures 12 1/2" x 12", and dates in the 1940s. *Courtesy of Rod Krupka.* $600

Shamrock Cloud Master Premium sign. Measures 10 1/2" x 12 1/2", and dates in the 1950s. *Courtesy of Rod Krupka.* $175

These Fill-em' Fast Gasoline signs are made from heavy gauge iron stock. However, they date to only the 1950s. Measures 16" x 9 1/2". *Courtesy of Rod Krupka.* $125

Sunray by D-X Petroleum Products die-cut sign. Their great-looking color scheme helps put this one on collector's "wanted" lists. Measures 8 1/2" across. These date from the 1930s. *Courtesy of Bob Knudsen Jr.* $1000

Any sign that has graphics like this Grizzly Gasoline sign is going to be super desirable! The bear was done using a silk screen process. Measures 12" in diameter, and dates in the 1930s. *Courtesy of Bob Knudsen Jr.* $1500

Here's the logo of the Ethyl Gasoline Corporation. These 8" diameter signs were used along side of hundreds of brand-name pump signs. This "early" Ethyl logo dates in the 1930s era, and was followed in the 1940s with a similar but modified version. *Courtesy of Rod Krupka. $75*

The Gasco Motor Fuel sign pictured here is rare. This company was bought out by Shell oil in the 1920s. Measures 12" in diameter. *Courtesy of Bob Knudsen Jr. $1700*

Veltex Gasoline sign. Measures 12 1/2" x 15", and dates in the 1940s. *Courtesy of Bob Knudsen Jr. $400*

This Energee! True Gasoline sign was curved to go on "visible" style pumps. Measures 15" in diameter, and dates in the 1920s. *Courtesy of Rod Krupka. $400*

This Golden Tip Gasoline sign was produced for the Stohl Oil Company of Kentucky. Also found in Lamp Oil and Diesel versions. All are rare. A pair of these is reportedly in service in the Louisville, Kentucky area. Measures 9" x 7" and dates in the 1940s. *Courtesy of Bob Knudsen Jr.* $650

These die-cut signs from The Atlantic Refining Company are referred to as the "fried egg" style. Measures 9" across, and dates around the 1930s. *Courtesy of John Bobroff.* $350

This Refiners Pride Gasoline sign features the "newer" style Ethyl logo. Measures 8" in diameter, and dates in the 1940s. *Courtesy of Bob Knudsen.* $750

The Standard Oil Products sign pictured here is rare. These small die-cut signs measure 12 1/2" x 6", and are from the 1930s era. *Courtesy of Bob Knudsen Jr.* $850

The Barnsdall Company produced this miniature sign in the 1920s. It measures only 3" in diameter. Its exact use is uncertain, but it possibly could have been used on oil pumps. *Courtesy of Rod Krupka.* $200

Texaco 10" diameter with a "black T." Marked at the bottom "3-31." *Courtesy of Bob Knudsen Jr.* $350

This Cities Service Oils sign is curved. It measures 11" in diameter, and dates around 1930. *Courtesy of Kim and Mary Kokles.* $300

This Vico Pep 88 Gasoline sign is from the 1930s. It measures 10" in diameter. *Courtesy of Bob Knudsen Jr.* $600

Signal Gasoline 12" diameter sign. Dates in the 1940s.
Courtesy of Bob Knudsen Jr. $900

Shamrock Trail Master Regular sign. Measures 10 1/2" x 13",
and dates from around 1950. *Courtesy of Rod Krupka.* $150

The 1960s saw several of the better known petroleum
companies boost their octane levels. However, few would go
to the extreme that Jetrol did with their unusual 100 plus
octane premium. Measures approximately 12" x 12". *Courtesy
of Rod Krupka.* $200

Chapter Six
A PORCELAIN POTPOURRI

Porcelain enamel advertising has come to mean substantially more than just signs. The list of items produced through the years could fill a book in itself.

Gum machines, pop dispensers, thermometers, ash trays, and a lot more all were produced with the common factor of having a porcelain message.

This unusual shaped Coca-Cola door push dates in the 1930s. It measures 35" x 4". Marked "REG US PAT OFF." *Courtesy of Dan Reynolds.* $350

Chew Pay Car door push. These measure 3" x 6", and date to around the 1920s. *Courtesy of John Bobroff.* $200

Jap Rose Soap is featured on this small door push. It measures approximately 4" x 11" and dates to around 1925. *Courtesy of Pete Keim.* $250

Farmers Mutual Liability Co. cloisonne. Measures 4 1/2" x 3", and dates around the 1950s. Embossed on the reverse "ROSS AD-SEAL INC. INDIANAPOLIS." *Author's collection.* $100

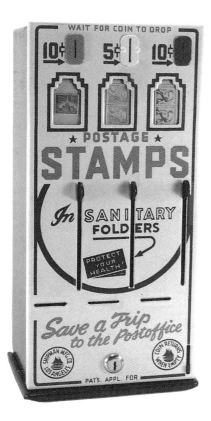

Many porcelain-faced stamp machines were produced through the years. This model by the Shipman Manufacturing Company of Los Angeles has the words "PROTECT YOUR HEALTH" on the front. Measures 7" x 16", and dates from around the 1940s. *Author's collection.* $125

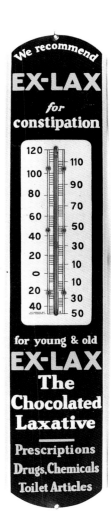

Ex-Lax was big on outside thermometers. This one measures 8" x 39", and is marked "PAT. MARCH 16, 1915 BEACH COSHOCTON, OHIO." *Courtesy of Dan Reynolds.* $400

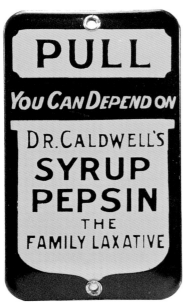

This Dr. Caldwell's porcelain door push actually says "PULL." This was meant to be placed near the handle of the door, and would still be called a door push by collectors. Measures 4" x 6 1/2", and dates around the 1920s. *Courtesy of Dan Reynolds.* $300

143

Hires produced this porcelain mixer for "milk drinks" around 1910. The lettering is the same on both sides, and is raised. Turning the crank would spin the rotor at the top center. Measures 10" at the base, and is 5" high. *Author's collection.* $3500

Many of the early gum machines used porcelain as an advertising medium. This Pulver machine dates from the 1920s era. It measures 8 1/2" x 20". *Courtesy of Bernie Nagel.* $850

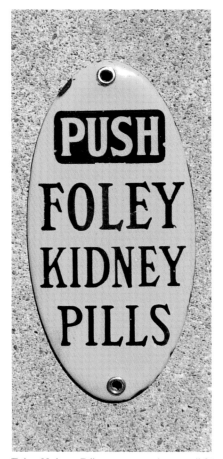

Foley Kidney Pills is seen on this small 3" x 6" oval door push. It dates from the 1920s. *Courtesy of Pete Keim.* $300

Porcelain advertising even shows up in the bathroom! The Boraxo soap dispenser pictured here measures 3 1/2" x 7 1/2", and dates around 1940. *Author's collection.* $125

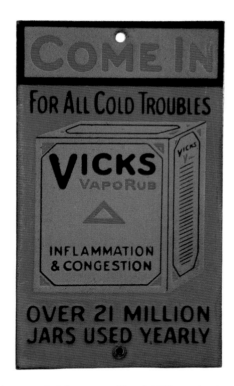

Vicks door push. Measures 4" x 6 1/2", and is from the 1930s. *Courtesy of John Bobroff.* $200

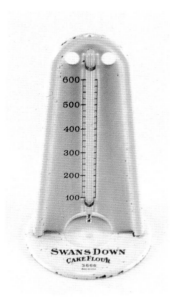

Swans Down Cake Flour oven thermometer. Many products used in the household were porcelain. Measures 3" x 5 1/2", and dates around the 1930s. *Courtesy of Rod Krupka.* $75

This Campbell's Merit Bread stand-up sign was used at lunch counters. The black area is a chalkboard. It measures 12" x 22", and dates from the 1930s era. Marked at the bottom "BURDICK, CHI." *Author's collection.* $1300

This Ex-Lax thermometer uses a round gauge instead of the usual tube. Measures 8" x 36". This one is from the 1920s. *Courtesy of Dan Reynolds.* $450

Ex-Lax thermometer. Again, the round gauge was employed instead of the usual tube. Measures 8" x 36". Dates around the 1920s. *Courtesy of Dan Reynolds.* $400

Sweeties Candy Thermometer. Measures 2" x 11 1/2". Dates in the 1940s. *Author's collection.* $75

Western Union produced many styles of call boxes. This model has the "globe" logo, which was in use at the turn of the century. You may recognize the initials at the top. They stand for American District Telegraph, a company which still survives today as manufacturers of alarm systems. Measures 3 1/2" x 6 1/2". *Courtesy of Dennis Weber.* $200

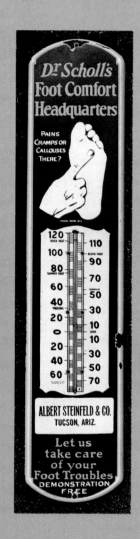

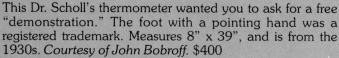

This Dr. Scholl's thermometer wanted you to ask for a free "demonstration." The foot with a pointing hand was a registered trademark. Measures 8" x 39", and is from the 1930s. *Courtesy of John Bobroff.* $400

These Piedmont Cigarette chairs were produced by the hundreds. However, few are around in this like-new condition. They date to the 1940s era. *Courtesy of Dan Reynolds.* $250

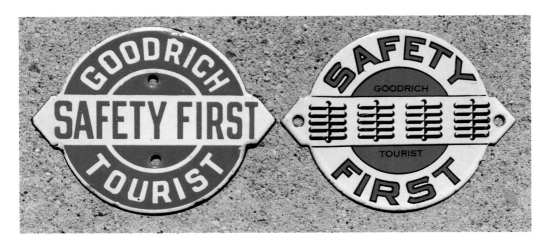

These two 4" diameter license plate tags were used in the era around 1925. No doubt they were given out when a set of new tires was purchased or when you belonged to the Goodrich Tourist club. *Courtesy of Dave Lowenthal.* $300 ea.

Swan Ice Cream sidewalk sign. This one was in storage for thirty years, and still has a like-new appearance. The stands are quite difficult to come by, as the elements often rusted them beyond usefulness. Measures approximately 35" x 22", and dates from the 1940s. *Author's collection.* $600

Campbell's Soup used this beautiful advertising thermometer in the 1920s. It measures 7 1/2" x 13". *Courtesy of Gary Metz.* $3800

Here's a scarce match striker advertising Coca-Cola. Measures only 4 1/2" x 4 1/2", this little beauty dates around the 1930s. *Courtesy of Dan Reynolds.* $500

Coca-Cola produced several styles and sizes of "button" signs over the years. This example with a white background and a bottle is one of the more scarce varieties. It measures 24" in diameter, and dates around the 1940s. *Courtesy of Jim Oswald.* $600

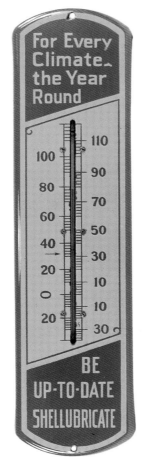

Shell petroleum used this scarce thermometer in the 1920s. It measures 7" x 27". *Courtesy of Dan Reynolds.* $1000

Enna Jettick Health Shoe counter top stand-up sign. Measures 10" x 6", and dates from the 1920s. *Author's collection.* $250

Here's another full width door push and bracket. The stripes at the ends are unusual. Measures 28" x 4", and dates from the 1930s. *Courtesy of Dan Reynolds.* $500

This is a side close-up of the Coca-Cola door push. The patent number refers to the design of the bracket, not the porcelain process.

This nifty case was made for General Electric to hold Mazda Super Auto Lamps. It measures 8" square by 15 1/2" high. A similar one is available with black, yellow and white porcelain. These date to the 1920s. *Author's collection.* $450

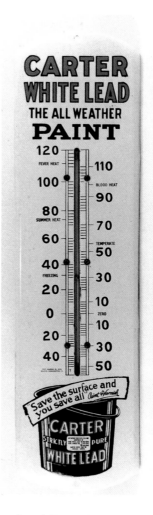

This Carter White Lead Paint thermometer dates from the 1920s. It measures 7 1/2" x 27". *Author's collection.* $350

The beautiful telephone pay station iron box shown here was recently discovered in a basement in Lafayette, Indiana. The left side has a sign that is identical to the one on the right side. The large center sign is one-of-a-kind. The entire box measures approximately 16" wide by 13" deep by 20" tall, and weighs in at around 90 pounds! It dates from the era around 1910. *Private Collection.* $5000

The R.G. Sullivan Cigar ash tray pictured has characteristics of those manufactured by Tennessee Enamel. It measures 5 1/2" in diameter, and would date in the 1930s. *Author's collection.* $60

Automobile Owners Association die-cut cloisonne. This colorful example dates in the 1940s. Measures 3" x 4 1/2". *Author's collection.* $75

This Lipton's Tea door push dates to around 1925. It measures approximately 3" x 9". *Courtesy of Pete Keim.* $300.

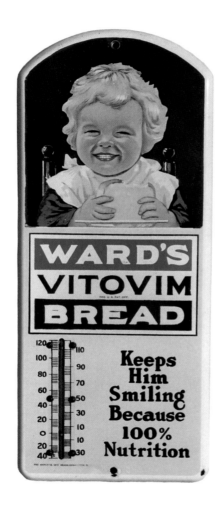

This outstanding Ward's Vitovim Bread thermometer dates to the 1920s. It measures 9" x 21", and is marked at the bottom "BEACH, COSHOCTON, O." *Author's Collection.* $1800.

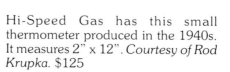

Hi-Speed Gas has this small thermometer produced in the 1940s. It measures 2" x 12". *Courtesy of Rod Krupka.* $125

As an aid to night viewing, signs were often manufactured with small reflectors, or "jewels" on the letters. In the 1920s many highway stop signs had these. This Public Telephone sign gives an idea how they look. Measures 36" x 18 1/2", and dates from around the 1930s. *Author's collection.* $500

These two Coca-Cola thermometers date from the 1940s. They measure 6" x 18". The one with the green center area is more scarce. *Courtesy of Dan Reynolds.* Left - $700, Right - $1100

Western Union used these wooden boxes in the early 1900s to hold telegraph blanks. The sign measures 9" x 4". *Courtesy of Dennis Weber.* $250

Here's a great display piece! This Vernor's Ginger Ale dispenser dates from the 1940s. It measures approximately 36" tall. *Private collection.* $1700

Ox-Heart Peanut Butter used this door push around 1910. It measures 4" x 8". *Private collection.* $600

Most everyone has spotted one of these still up on an old store. As numerous as these were at one time, they are getting difficult to spot any more. The one here, of course, is made of porcelain. However, similar appearing ones were baked enamel (painted). The painted ones had a tendency to fade. The one pictured here measures 24" in diameter, but they were made with identical graphics in smaller as well as larger sizes. *Courtesy of Dan Reynolds.* $450

Zeno Gum, like many early advertisers, made use of every inch of space to carry their message. Large arched letters with serifs gave the desired impact. Not to be forgotten, the word "ZENO" appears no less than seven times on this machine! Measures 7" x 5 1/2" x 16", and dates from the 1910 era. *Courtesy of Bernie Nagel.* $750

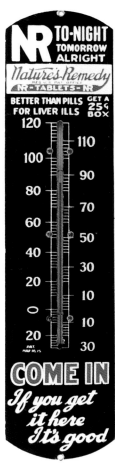

Nature's Remedy thermometer. Measures 7 1/2" x 27". Dates around the 1920s. *Author's collection.* $350

This Moehn Brewing Company "hubcap" style sign was produced around 1910. It must have been a stencil maker's nightmare to get through this one! But as you can see, the end result was worth it. Measures 17 1/2" in diameter. *Author's collection.* $1850

Crystal White Soap is featured on this 3" x 9" door push. It dates from the 1920s. *Courtesy of Pete Keim.* $150.

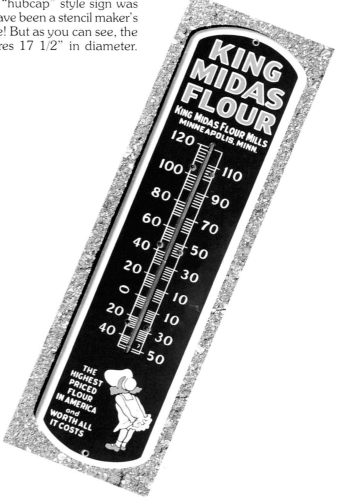

King Midas Flour used this neat thermometer in the 1920s. It measures 7" x 27". *Author's Collection.* $1500.

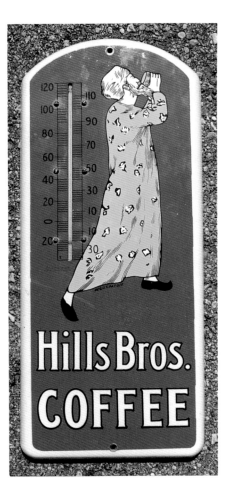

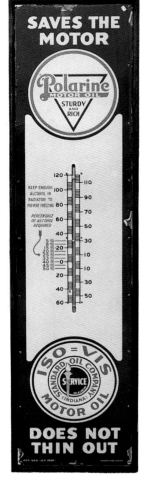

A box of Star Naphtha Washing Powder is seen on this door push dating from the 1920s. It measures approximately 6" x 10". *Courtesy of Pete Keim.* $500.

Standard Oil Company used these large six-foot-tall thermometers on stations. They could also be found doing service at other locations such as stores, restaurants or anywhere the public might frequent. Dates in the 1920s. Marked at the bottom "VERIBRITE SIGNS, CHICAGO." *Courtesy of Ben Weaver.* $850

These Hills Brothers Coffee thermometers are scarce in such outstanding condition. Measures 9" x 21", and dates from the 1920s. era. *Private Collection.* $700.

Magic Yeast door push. Measures 3" x 5", and dates in the 1930s. *Courtesy of Viking Antiques.* $200

This Abbott's Bitters thermometer dates around 1910. The volcano screw holes place the manufacturer as Ingram-Richardson. Measures 6" x 29". Possibly of equal interest is the paper label affixed to the back, as shown on the accompanying photograph. *Courtesy of Dave Lowenthal.* $1100

This Lash's Bitters sign had the unusual job of doubling as a cigar holder. The words "AT THE BAR" placed at the bottom of the sign indicates its possible use as being found in the gentlemen's restroom. It measures approximately 5" x 9" and dates from around 1925. *Courtesy of Pete Keim.* $350.

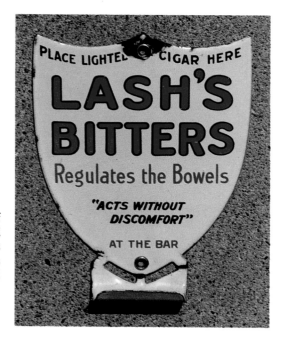

158

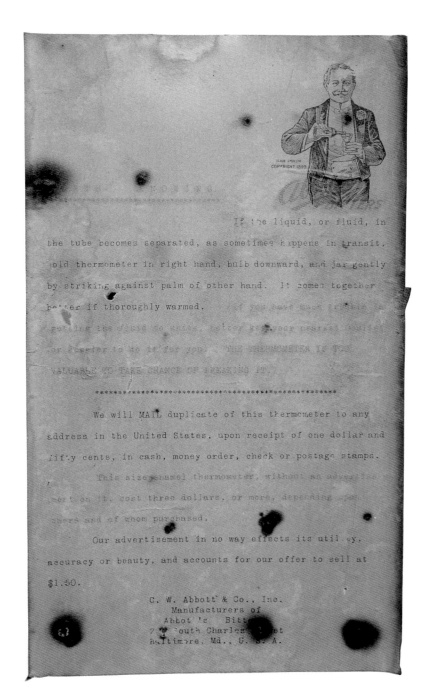

This label is on the back side of the Abbott's thermometer. It reads: WORTH KNOWING: *If the liquid or fluid in the tube becomes separated, as sometimes happens in transit, hold thermometer in right hand bulb downward, and jar gently by striking against palm of other hand. It comes together better if thoroughly warmed. If you have much trouble in getting the fluid to unite, better get your nearest Oculist or Jeweler to do it for you.* THE THERMOMETER IS TOO VALUABLE TO TAKE CHANCE ON BREAKING IT.

We will MAIL duplicate of this thermometer to any address in the United States, upon receipt of one dollar and fifty cents, in cash, money order, check or postage stamps.

This size thermometer, without any advertisement on it, cost three dollars, or more, depending upon where and of whom purchased.

Our advertisement in no way effects its utility, accuracy or beauty, and accounts for our offer to sell at $1.50.

Chapter Seven

NEON PORCELAIN SIGNS

As neon lighting came into widespread use in the 1930s, it was used in combination with porcelain advertising. This type of sign had all the regular benefits of porcelain enamel to be seen in daylight, and could come alive at night. Many of these relics from the past are still in service today, most notably on theaters.

This 24" diameter OK neon was from the used car lot at a Chevrolet dealership. Dates in the 1950s. *Courtesy of Bob Knudsen Jr.* $900

Red Goose Shoes neon. This unmistakable trade mark is shown on a dismantled outside display. Note the two large holes allowing the former neon tubing to pass through the sign front. Measures 24" x 36", and dates from the 1940s. *Courtesy of Larry Schrof.* $1100

Here's a Blatz die-cut neon porcelain sign. A few of these are still found on old-time taverns. It measures approximately 7' x 3', and dates in the 1930s. This one says "ARTCRAFT NEON" at the bottom. *Courtesy of Ted Tear.* $1500

United Motors Service oval sign. These date to the 1930s, and measure approximately 48" across. This one was manufactured by Walker & Co., Detroit. *Author's collection.* $1400

The Case eagle pictured here has an identical sign behind it that is separated by an eight-inch spacer. Measures 18" x 40", and dates from the 1930s. *Courtesy of Rody Cummings.* $1000

Rexall Drugstores were frequently appointed with these large "mural" type porcelain fronts. Each section of the large wall sign measures approximately 4' x 5', and eleven of them were needed here! The oval neon sign was porcelain as well, and measures approximately 8' x 6'. These date from the 1930s, and to this day many can still be found in service. The one photographed here is still up in Marshall, Michigan.

Hundreds of theaters used large porcelain marquees. The one pictured here has a colorful Indian motif, and a couple hundred feet of neon tubing. The "Wapa" is still going strong in Wapakoneta, Ohio.

Most small American towns had such amenities as a local automobile dealership and service center. This Ford sign was found still giving faithful service in Mayville, Michigan. The man on the street seems perplexed as to what has caught my interest.

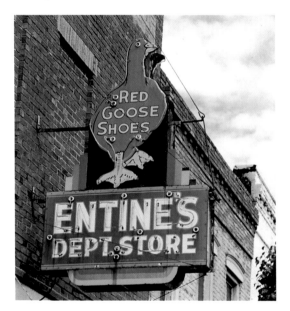

Like most other well-recognized trademarks, this Red Goose Shoes sign is seldom found today. The one here stands as a reminder of days gone by in Lexington, Missouri.

The Columbia Bank neon shown here would not be much of an attention-getter without the fabulous "Miss Columbia" and eagle included. She measures about life-size. The colors are absolutely vivid when viewed in bright sunlight! She stands in full glory in Ybor City, Florida.

Chapter Eight
PORCELAIN ENAMEL MANUFACTURING

Many admirers of porcelain enamel advertising never give a second thought to the processes that were involved in its manufacture. This is unfortunate, as a wealth of information is to be found in the companies that produced porcelain enamel through the years. To realize that there were hundreds of companies producing porcelain enamel gives one an idea as to the immense industry that developed from a need to make the most durable form of advertising.

The origins of porcelain enamel are not know. Relics of early civilizations in Asia have been unearthed with artifacts of porcelain enamel. So our ancestors had already developed a knowledge of porcelain and its manufacture long before it became the exact science we know today.

The earliest advertising in porcelain enamel originated in Europe. England was one of the first countries to develop porcelain advertising, with production going back to around 1880. Indeed, many of the first porcelain signs used in the United States were actually manufactured in England. Two of the most prevalent English companies were Patent Enamel of Selly Oak, and Imperial Enamel of Birmingham. Many of the skilled artisans needed to get production established in America were from England and Germany.

The first company known to manufacturing porcelain enamel advertising in the United States was Hartman Steel Company of Ellwood City, Pennsylvania. They were established in 1887, but their tenure was short-lived as production ceased in 1890. During this same early time period the Patent Enamel Company Limited of Selly Oak, England, established a branch in Ellwood City, Pennsylvania. This company ceased production after one year; their employees dispersing to various American enamelers. Within two years another company got its start in nearby Beaver Falls, Pennsylvania. They were called "Enameled Iron Company". This small beginning giant known as Ingram-Richardson in the year 1901.

In 1897 another giant emerged, the Baltimore Enamel Company, which was to become three times as large as Ingram-Richardson and produced literally millions of enameled signs.

By 1920 the United States was far and away the world's largest producer of enameled signs. There were hundreds of enameling works including many huge companies such as California Metal Enameling Company (CAMEO), General Porcelain Enamel & Manufacturing Company (Veribrite) and the Tennessee Enamel Manufacturing Company.

The actual processes involved in the manufacturing of porcelain enamel are not complicated, and every collector should have a basic understanding of how porcelain enamel is made. This will give you and appreciation of the work involved in production, and it will enhance your ability to correctly date a sign.

There were more than a dozen ingredients used in the production of porcelain enamel. Some of the raw materials were imported. As a first step in production of porcelain enamel, these materials were mixed and then placed into a smelter. This took the mixture to a temperature around two thousand degrees. Upon completion of heating, the molten mass was dumped into bins filled with cold water. The contrast in the temperature of the water caused the mixture to shatter into millions of small pieces. This granulated compound was called "frit."

The frit was allowed to dry and was then passed through a magnetic separator. This removed any iron impurities that would cause the finished product to be discolored. The frit was the material that would eventually become the finished surface of porcelain enamel.

After the frit was separated into bins according to the size of the granules, it was ground into a powder-like substance with the help of water, clay and other ingredients. Metallic oxides were added for color variations, and then the fine powdered frit was dried.

Ingram Richardson Celebrated their 50th anniversary in 1951. To help draw attention to this milestone, a commemorative ash tray was produced. Note the modified logo. *Courtesy of Dennis Weber.* $150

In advertising the porcelain enamel was fused to a metal base. The early years of manufacture saw the use of rolled iron as the most common metal base for porcelain signs. Around 1920 most of the producers were switching to steel. This was superior for its stable properties under the high temperatures required to fuse the porcelain.

The metal base needed to be shaped to the desired size. This would involve die-cutting any needed pattern, drilling holes for mounting supports and, if needed, putting the metal on a "break" to create a flange.

After these steps were taken, the metal piece would go into a "pickling" bath. A solution of mild acids was used to remove dirt, grease and other impurities from the metal. The metal blank was then ready to have porcelain fired to its surface.

All porcelain products required a preliminary "ground coat" to be fired first at approximately two thousand degrees. This set up the metal for the regular applications of porcelain and the successive trips through the kiln. A stenciled sign with four colors would have required five trips through the firing kiln! Each successive coating added to the thickness of the porcelain. This gave the areas along the edges of two colors the feeling of being built up, a process that collectors call "shelving".

In the years prior to 1930, the most common method of creating a design employed the use of a "stencil". This was normally made of sheet brass, and had the desired pattern "cut out" by a fabricating machine. Sometimes several stencils were required in the production of one sign, each responsible for a separate color.

The use of the stencil is often misunderstood. The stencil was used to create a pattern by removing the powder from areas not to be colored. The powdered frit was sprayed on the entire surface of the sign. This left the sign as if you took a can of spray paint and covered the whole thing. The frit had a very slight adhesive property to it. This prevented it from being dusted off the sign while it was being handled. However, it still could be removed by something like a hand brush with little effort.

After this spray coating is applied, the cut-out stencil is placed on the sign's surface. With the use of a small hand-held brush, a worker would go over the surface of the stencil. Any areas of the frit that were under the stencil's "cut-out" pattern would be "brushed" out. When the stencil was lifted off the face of the sign the cut-out area would have the sprayed-on frit removed.

At this time the sign went into a firing kiln. The temperatures involved in fusing porcelain were in the range of sixteen hundred degrees. The furnaces used were large and employed a conveyor system. Once through the kiln the powdered frit became fused to the base material. The sign was allowed to cool and would then be ready for additional coatings of frit. Each application required a different stencil, and each stencil was responsible for a different color.

The other major technique employed in the manufacture of porcelain enamel was the use of a silk screen. Although the stencil proved to withstand long term hard use, the economy involved in the production of silk screens, combined with simplified use, made stencils obsolete by around 1930.

Manufacturers have used silk screens for porcelain enamel production since the turn of the century. This method involves using a framed screen to apply the colors. The area not to be covered would be filled in so that only the open areas of the screen became part of the sign's image.

The use of silk screens in the production of porcelain enamel gave the edges of contrasting colors a "rough" edge. This is in contrast with the smooth lines found on stenciled signs. These rough edges were the result of the mesh of the screen, and with close examination you may be able to see the screen's woven pattern in other places. The use of silk screens reduced the amount of shelving on contrasting colors and signs produced after 1940 will have almost no shelving.

Lithography is another method by which images were created on a porcelain enameled sign. This method was used to achieve the greatest detail—far greater than could be obtained by the stenciling process. Lithographed images on porcelain enamel signs were at their peak of usage in the 1900–1915 period.

Lithography involves the transferring of porcelain enamel onto a decal which is then applied to

This is a test plate from McMath-Axilrod Corporation. It measures 10" x 12", and dates in the 1950s. *Courtesy of Bob Alexander.* $50

the metal base. The image is created on a stone or zinc plate with a greasy crayon. By wetting the surface with a squeegee and applying the porcelain-based "ink" to the plate only the areas drawn in with the crayon will form an image.

The lithographic processes developed in Germany for the application of porcelain enamel employed the use of stippling (small dots) to form various depths of colors and shadings.

Hopefully this brief chapter on porcelain enamel manufacturing has provided some idea as to the processes involved in production. As you become a "seasoned" collector, you will find that knowing the processes can be a very helpful tool in the identification and evaluation of porcelain enamel advertising.

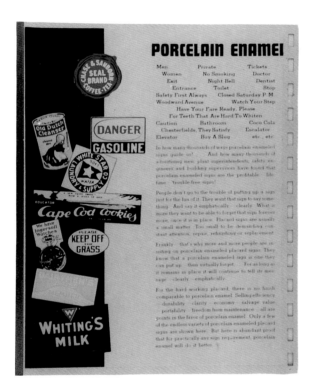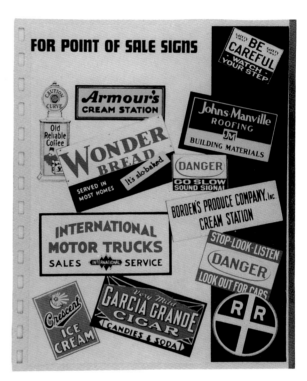

This two page spread from a Baltimore Enamel catalog shows the customer a few of the possibilities to be found in porcelain enamel advertising.

This is an advertising piece from Porcelain Metals Incorporated. It measures 16" x 10", and appears to be from the 1940s era. *Courtesy of Bob Alexander.* $250

"Psychedelic" might be a good word to describe this Ingram Richardson advertising sign from the 1930s era. It measures 8 1/2" x 11". *Courtesy of Bob Alexander.* $500

Baltimore Enamel & Novelty Company had these color samples made so that a customer could "see" how their sign would look before they committed to a manufacturing contract. As indicated by the sample numbers, it would appear that at least three hundred sixty nine sample colors were made. About forty of these nifty little plates turned up at an auction recently, these being the only ones found so far. Each measures 2 1/2" x 5", and date to around the 1920s. *Author's collection.* $30 ea.

This may be the largest porcelain manufacturing company advertising sign ever made! It measures 27 1/2" x 60", and dates around the 1930s. *Courtesy of Bob Alexander.* $700

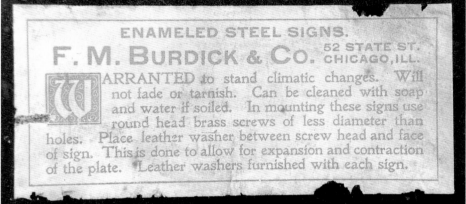

The Texas Neon Advertising Company. Measures 7" x 7". This dates around 1950. *Courtesy of Bob Alexander.* $50

Photographed here is a specimen of a paper decal found on the back of a sign manufactured by F.M. Burdick & Co. Note that there is a mention of "leather washers." These certainly rotted away in time as none seem to have survived. The decal measures 2" x 6". *Courtesy of John Bobroff.*

This cities Service Test Plate is from an unknown manufacturer. It measures 5" x 7". *Courtesy of Bob Alexander.* $75

Baltimore Enamel made this advertisement around the 1930s. Note that Mt. Winans was listed as one of their locations. Measures 21" x 29 1/2". *Courtesy of Bob Alexander.* $1300

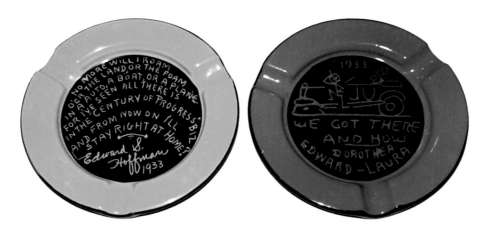

As a promotional maneuver, the Porcelain Enamel Institute set up a display booth at the 1933 Century Of Progress Worlds Fair. The two ash trays pictured here were from this exhibition. It appears that a small firing kiln was set up right at the fair, and curious visitors could have the opportunity of making their own porcelain souvenir. No doubt the base color was already pre-fired, allowing the happy fair goer to select the desired color. These measure approximately 5" in diameter. *Courtesy of Rody Cummings.* $75 ea.

The back of each ash tray had a felt "coaster" attached to it. The small print reads "cleanliness and beauty" and "fused on metal." *Courtesy of Rody Cummings.*

Industrial Signs Inc. Measures 13" x 5", and is from the 1960s era. *Courtesy of Bob Alexander.* $50

It's hard to imagine this 5" x 2 1/2" piece of paper still being fastened to the back of a sign that's eighty five years old. These labels are quite scarce, and should be given careful handling to keep them intact. *Courtesy of Dan Reynolds.*

This 5" round ash tray from Ingram-Richardson dates around 1915. *Courtesy of Dennis Weber.* $150

This beautiful ING-RICH advertising sign measures 6" x 9", and dates around 1910. *Courtesy of Bob Alexander.* $700

Here's a rare advertising piece from Ing-Rich. It measures 3" x 6", and dates around 1915. *Courtesy of Bob Alexander.* $700

169

The Chicago Vitreous Enamel Product Company was located in Cicero, Illinois. This piece dates around 1930, and measures 18" x 12". *Courtesy of Bob Alexander.* $275

The presentation plaque shown here was no doubt made in honor of Dr. J.S. Louthan's retirement. The list of officials includes both Ernest Richardson and Fred Ingram. It measures 11" x 14", and dates in the 1930s era. *Courtesy of Bob Alexander.* $300

Porcelain Enamel Manufacturing Company had this backboard made for holding a calendar in the 1950s. Measures 8 1/2" x 12 1/2". *Courtesy of Bob Alexander.* $300

Wisconsin Creameries Ice Cream sign measures approximately 27" x 20" and is flat one-sided and dates to the 1930s. *Author's Collection.* $450

Sugar Creek Creamery Company die-cut flanged sign featuring a one-pound package of butter. The sign measures approximately 22" x 17". Not to be ignored, Nesco Inc. made sure their name was placed prominently at the bottom right. Dates from the 1930s. *Author's Collection.* $550

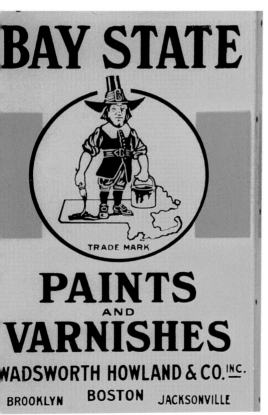

Aztec Manufacturing Company used appropriate graphics on this 13" x 4" flat one-sided sign. Its exact use is uncertain. However, it apparently was manufactured in 1957. *Author's Collection.* $200

Bay State Paints and Varnishes was headquartered in Boston, Massachusetts. This flanged sign features a whimsical pilgrim ready to paint the entire state. It measures approximately 14" x 24" and dates to around 1935. *Author's Collection.* $800

Ingram-Richardson came up with the novel idea of a wood-grained background on this Dutchess Trousers flanged sign dating from around 1920. The sign measures approximately 16" x 11" and is featured in an early Ingram-Richardson catalog. *Author's Collection.* $900

Here's a close-up of the superb workmanship produced by Ingram-Richardson on the Allegheny Fire Insurance sign. It shows an American Indian paddling his canoe past a log cabin.

Anheuser-Busch found a profitable way to wait out their time during prohibition. While many breweries simply ceased operation during those times, Anheuser-Busch began to produce thirst quenchers in a non-alcoholic variety as can be seen on this Busch Extra Dry Ginger Ale sign. It is flat, one-sided, and measures approximately 22" x 12". *Author's Collection.* $850

This Stroh's Lager Beer tray was manufactured sometime around 1895. It is made of brass with a porcelain insert and measures approximately 13" in diameter. *Author's Collection.* $900

By the early 1900s insurance companies were doing big business. Although this Allegheny Fire Insurance Company sign was manufactured in only two colors, its outstanding log cabin graphics put it in a class by itself. It is flat, one-sided, and measures approximately 18" x 15". *Author's Collection.* $750

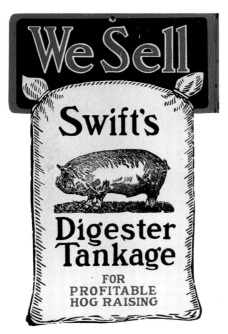

This outstanding die-cut Swift's Meat Scraps sign has some great country graphics. The sign featured here presents a healthy looking hen ready to do her job filling the egg basket. Flanged, two-sided, measures approximately 22" x 32". *Author's Collection.* $1350

The reverse side of the die-cut Swift's sign features a rather rotund hog giving you his best pose.

This American Telephone & Telegraph convex sign was designed to be placed on phone booths. Although similar in nature to some of the other telephone signs, these booth signs are rare. It measures approximately 8" x 10" and dates from around 1910. *Author's Collection.* $1000

Cressman's Counsellor Five Cent Cigar circa 1915. Measures 4" x 8.5". *Courtesy of Pete Keim.* Scarce

J & B Coffee flat one-sided sign from around 1930. Measures approximately 13" x 24" *Courtesy of Pete Keim.* Scarce

This wonderful little cup was no doubt used as a scoop to dispense seed. It features graphics on each side with Pine Tree Timothy Seed being seen here. This item dates to probably around 1910. *Author's Collection.* $150

Worden's Ice Cream dates from approximately 1915 and measures 3" x 7". *Courtesy of Pete Keim* $300

Left: Here's the opposite side of the Dickenson's Cup advertises Ace Clover.

Right: How's this for color? As best as we can tell, this Union Nursery sign has 17 colors! But who's counting? At any rate, it's one of the most colorful porcelain signs to be found anywhere. It is flat, one-sided and dates from the 1940s. It is made in two sections and is not silk-screened but stenciled throughout. Measures approximately 36" x 24". *Courtesy of Pete Keim.* Scarce.

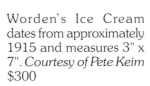

MANUFACTURERS

The following is a listing of the manufacturers names that are found on the signs in this book. Most of the major companies will be present as they produced high quantities of signs. Street addresses are not listed because some companies did business at more than one location.

Many of the companies listed were manufacturers of very different porducts, such as stove casings, building panels, kitchen ware, and other utilitarian items. Although it is difficult to establish, the dates listed will give you an idea as to a particular company's "heyday". A (*) designates that limited informatin is available for the years of production.

It is of interest to note that one of the most frequently encountered names found on signs, F.M. BURDICK, of Chicago, was a distributor, not a manufacturer. This will be true of a few of the other companies as well.

ACTON BURROWS CO., TORONTO, CANADA, 1900-1920

AMERICAN SIGN COMPANY, 1920-1930

AMERICAN VALVE & ENAMELING CORP., 1928-1970

BALTIMORE ENAMEL, BALTIMORE, MARYLAND, 1897-1943

BEACH, COSHOCTON, OHIO, 1910-1940

BEATTY McMILLAN CO., DETROIT, MICHIGAN, (*)

BILLY NEWTON COMPANY, MINNESOTA, 1930-1940

BRILLIANT MANUFACTURING CO., PHILADELPHIA, PENNSYLVANIA, 1910-1930

BURDICK, CHICAGO, ILLINOIS, 1895-1950

C. ROBERT DOLD, OFFENBURG, GERMANY, 1905-1920

CAMEO GILA, 1904-1980

CHICAGO VITREOUS ENAMEL PRODUCT COMPANY, 1930-1980

CRICHTON CURL ENAMEL CO., ELLWOOD CITY, PENNSYLVANIA, 1905-1920

ENAMELED IRON CO., BEAVER FALLS, PENNSYLVANIA, 1892-1900

ENAMELED STEEL SIGN CO., CHICAGO, ILLINOIS, 1900-1920

F. FRANCIS AND SONS LTD., LONDON, S.E., (*)

F.E. MARSLAND, NY HARTMAN (STEEL CO.

OF ELLWOOD CITY, PENNSYLVANIA), 1890-1910

IMPERIAL ENAMEL CO. LTD., NEW YORK, 1890-1910

INDUSTRIAL SIGNS INCORPORATED, 1940-1950

INGRAM-RICHARDSON, BEAVER FALLS, PENNSYLVANIA, 1901-1960

L.D. NELKE SIGNS, NEW YORK, 1900-1935

MARYLAND ENAMEL & SIGN CO., BALTIMORE, MARYLAND, 1900-1920

MC MATH AXILROD, DALLAS, TEXAS, 1930-1965

MULHOLLAND, PHILADELPHIA, PENNSYLVANIA, 1925-1940

NATIONAL ENAMELING CO., CINCINNATI, OHIO, 1895-1915

NESCO INC. SIGNS, NEW YORK & TOLEDO, OHIO (*)

ORME EVANS & CO. LTD., NEW YORK, 1895-1915

P & M, ORILLA, ONTARIO, CANADA, 1930-1950

PENNSYLVANIA ENAMEL, NEW CASTLE, PENNSYLVANIA, (*)

PORCELAIN ENAMEL MANUFACTURING COMPANY, 1910-1950

PORCELAIN METALS INCORPORATED, 1925-1950

RELIANCE ADVERTISING CO., NEW YORK, 1915-1930

SALES SERVICE CORPORATION, CHICAGO, ILLINOIS, 1920-1930

SHANK SIGN CO., NEW YORK, 1920-1930

TENNESSEE ENAMEL MANUFACTURING CO., NASHVILLE, TENNESSEE, 1925-1970

TEXAS NEON ADVERTISING COMPANY, 1940-1950

TEXLITE, DALLAS, TEXAS, 1920-1960

VERIBRITE SIGNS, CHICAGO, ILLINOIS, 1915-1965

W.F. VILAS CO. LTD., COWANSVILLE, F.C., 1925-1950

WALKER & COMPANY, DETROIT, MICHIGAN, 1925-1960

WOLVERINE PORCELAIN, DETROIT, MICHIGAN, 1925-1945

Like any prominent manufacturer, ING-RICH found that well-illustrated catalogs were a productive way to market their products. The pages shown here are from a promotional catalog dating to around 1935. *Courtesy of The Resource & Research Center for Beaver Falls, Pennsylvania.*

INGRAM-RICHARDSON MFG. CO., BEAVER FALLS, PENNA.

Ing-Rich Signs are used to advertise many well known products in the automotive fields

1	30 x 14	Double Face	Two Colors
2	32 x 12½	Double Face	Three Colors
3	48 x 18	Single Face	Three Colors
4	30 x 16	Double Face	Two Colors
5	40 x 28	Double Face	Three Colors
6	40 x 28	Double Face	Two Colors
7	24 x 72	Single Face Cut Out	Three Colors
8	216 x 36	Single Face	Three Colors

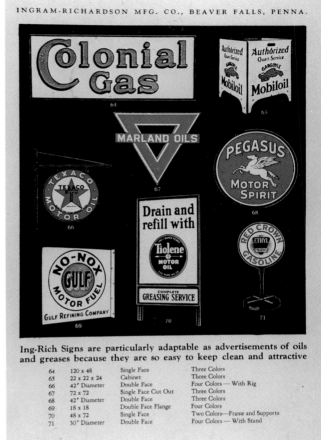

INGRAM-RICHARDSON MFG. CO., BEAVER FALLS, PENNA.

Ing-Rich Signs are particularly adaptable as advertisements of oils and greases because they are so easy to keep clean and attractive

64	120 x 48	Single Face	Three Colors
65	22 x 22 x 24	Cabinet	Three Colors
66	42" Diameter	Double Face	Four Colors — With Rig
67	72 x 72	Single Face Cut Out	Three Colors
68	42" Diameter	Double Face	Three Colors
69	18 x 18	Double Face Flange	Four Colors
70	48 x 72	Single Face	Two Colors—Frame and Supports
71	30" Diameter	Double Face	Four Colors — With Stand

INGRAM-RICHARDSON MFG. CO., BEAVER FALLS, PENNA.

Your own grocery store probably displays at least one Ing-Rich Sign installed by some far-seeing manufacturer.

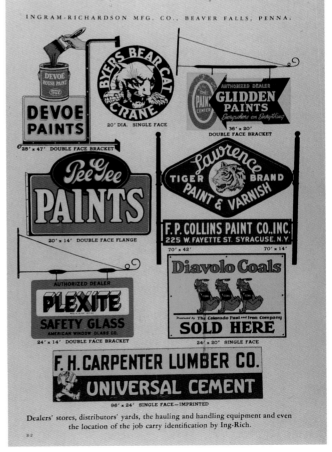

INGRAM-RICHARDSON MFG. CO., BEAVER FALLS, PENNA.

Dealers' stores, distributors' yards, the hauling and handling equipment and even the location of the job carry identification by Ing-Rich.

GLOSSARY

The following words are frequently encountered in collecting porcelain enamel advertising.

BRACKET: A supporting device for a sign, normally made from flat and bar stock iron and constructed by hand.

BRUSH MARKS: The slight lines of fired-on frit that can be seen on many stenciled signs. These were the result of not "brushing" out all the area of a stencil.

BUTTON SIGN: Those signs that have the shape of a button; most notably those round Coca-Cola signs of the 1940s and 1950s.

CLOISONNÉ: A multi-colored sign, using metal partitions to separate colors. These are normally small advertising pieces such as emblems, badges or buttons.

CORNER SIGN: Any sign that was designed to be displayed on the corner of a building by employing a special supporting bracket.

CRAZING: The appearance of fine cracks in the porcelain's finish. These will not have a uniform look, and are caused by the manufacturer not allowing proper cooling after running the sign through the kiln.

DECAL: The application of a lithographed paper to a sign's surface to be fired on. This was done in cases that proved too complicated for a silk screen or stencil.

DIE-CUT: A shape or form that is cut with a die powered by a press. Any sign that is not square, rectangular, circular or oval has a "die-cut" design by definition.

ETCHED: The loss of natural shine in porcelain. This is normally caused by chemicals in the atmosphere and/or by long-term exposure to a grounded surface.

EYELET: A single ring-like device, normally made of brass that was pressed into the mounting hole openings. This offered protection to the porcelain on one side.

FIRED: The process of heating metal and porcelain to the temperature required for fusing to occur, normally around 1600 degrees.

FLANGE: The area on a sign that is formed at ninety degrees to allow fastening to a wall.

GRAPHICS: The art work or design pattern on a sign.

GROMMET: A pair of washer-like rings, normally made of brass that were designed to be pressed together as protection against chips from the mounting screws. These offered protection on both sides of a sign and were most often found on hanging type signs.

HUB-CAP: A round convex sign.

INK-STAMPED: A process of applying ink with a rubber stamp. The ink would be fired on in a kiln. Most commonly used to identify a manufacturer and address.

KILN: The high temperature furnace used to fire on porcelain.

LITHOGRAPHIC TRANSFER: Applying detailed images on porcelain by the use of a decal.

LOGO: The design or emblem used to represent a company's product or services. As an example, the "gargoyle" was a logo used by Mobil Oil.

ROLLED IRON: The process of "drawing" iron through a set of rollers to increase its strength. Mostly in use before steel could be made inexpensively.

SANS-SERIF: Lettering that is in "block" form.

SELF-FRAMED: Any sign that has a raised border to set off the design on the sign's inside.

SERIF: Lettering that has the ends made with a "stylish" flair.

SHELVING: Used to describe the effect of layering caused by successive layers of porcelain being fired one on top of the other. This will produce a "ridge" of porcelain at places where different colors border each other.

SILK SCREEN: A silk or synthetic screen, used to apply frit to a sign's surface.

SPLIT FLANGE: A sign that was made with its ninety degree mounting done in two opposite directions.

STENCIL: A metallic sheet, usually made of brass, that was used to create lettering or a design. The intended pattern was cut out of the sheet, and this was placed on the sign's surface after frit was applied. The surface of the stencil was then "brushed", eliminating the frit on the exposed cutout areas.

STRESS CRACKS: Hairline cracks in porcelain that are due to stresses created in use, most often from repeated battering by high winds.

STRIP SIGN: A sign that will measure considerably greater in width than height, long enough that the word "rectangle" does not describe its shape.

VITRIFIED: To change into a glass-like substance by means of heat and fusion.

VOLCANO SCREW HOLE: The screw holes found in a sign that have a raised inner ridge. This design was patented by Ingram Richardson in 1907.

Here's a photograph of the stencil cutting and layout room at the ING-RICH plant around 1930. These gentlemen are busy drafting sketches for the stencil making process. Notice just a few "odds & ends" laying around the shop that might be of interest to today's collector! *Courtesy of The Resource & Research Center for Beaver Falls, Pennsylvania.*